SOLUTIONS MANUAL
for Even-Numbered Problems

to accompany

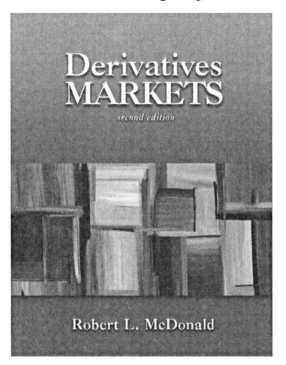

Mark Cassano
University of Calgary

Rüdiger Fahlenbrach
Fisher College of Business
The Ohio State University

Boston San Francisco New York
London Toronto Sydney Tokyo Singapore Madrid
Mexico City Munich Paris Cape Town Hong Kong Montreal

Practice Problems and Solutions to Accompany McDonald, *Derivatives Markets*, 2nd Edition

Copyright © 2006 Pearson Education, Inc.

ISBN 0-321-28647-2
         8 9 10-OPM-09 08

Table of Contents

Chapter 1
Introduction to Derivatives

Question 1.2.

A variety of counter-parties are imaginable. For one, we could think about speculators who have differences in opinion and who do not believe that we will have excessive temperature variations during the life of the futures contracts. Thus, they are willing to take the opposing side, receiving a payoff if the weather is stable.

Alternatively, there may be opposing hedging needs: Compare the ski-resort operator and the soft-drink manufacturer, The cooling degree-day futures contract will pay off if it the weather is relatively mild, and we saw that the resort operator will buy the futures contract. The buyer of the cooling degree-day futures will make a loss if the weather is cold (which means that the seller of the contract will make a gain). Since the soft drink manufacturer wants additional money if it is cold, she may be interested in taking the opposite side of the cooling degree-day futures.

Question 1.4.

In this problem, the brokerage fee is variable, and depends on the actual dollar amount of the sale/purchase of the shares. The concept of the transaction cost remains the same: If you buy the shares, the commission is added to the amount you owe, and if you sell the shares, the commission is deducted from the proceeds of the sale.

a)
$$(\$41.05 \times 100) + (\$41.05 \times 100) \times 0.003 = \$4,117.315$$
$$= \$4,117.32$$

b)
$$(\$40.95 \times 100) - (\$40.95 \times 100) \times 0.003 = \$4,082.715$$
$$= \$4,082.72$$

c)
$$\$4,117.32 - \$4,082.72 = \$34.6$$

The variable (or proportional) brokerage fee is advantageous to us. Our round-trip transaction fees are reduced by \$15.40.

Question 1.6.

A short sale of XYZ entails borrowing shares of XYZ and then selling them, receiving cash. Therefore, initially, we will receive the proceeds from the sale of the asset, less the proportional commission charge:

$$300 \times (\$30.19) - 300 \times (\$30.19) \times 0.005 = \$9,057 \times 0.995$$
$$= \$9,011.72$$

When we close out the position, we will again incur the commission charge, which is added to the purchasing cost:

$$300 \times (\$29.87) + 300 \times (\$29.87) \times 0.005 = \$8,961 \times 1.005$$
$$= \$9,005.81$$

Finally, we subtract the cost of covering the short position from our initial proceeds to receive total profits: $\$9,011.72 - \$9,005.81 = \$5.91$. We can see that the commission charge that we have to pay twice significantly reduces the profits we can make.

Question 1.8.

We learned from the main text that short selling is equivalent to borrowing money, and that a short seller will often have to deposit the proceeds of the short sale with the lender as collateral.

A short seller is entitled to earn interest on his collateral, and the interest rate he earns is called the short rebate in the stock market. Usually, the short rebate is close to the prevailing market interest rate. Sometimes, though, a particular stock is scarce and difficult to borrow. In this case, the short rebate is substantially less than the current market interest rate, and an equity lender can earn a nice profit in the form of the difference between the current market interest rate and the short rebate.

By signing an agreement as mentioned in the problem, you give your brokerage firm the possibility to act as an equity lender, using the shares of your account. Brokers want you to sign such an agreement because they can make additional profits.

Question 1.10.

The following information on short interest comes from NASDAQ's market data Internet site (http://www.marketdata.nasdaq.com). They explain:

> **How is short interest in Nasdaq stocks calculated?**
> *Short selling is the selling of a security which the seller does not own, or any sale which is completed by the delivery of a security borrowed by the seller. Short selling is a legitimate trading strategy. Short sellers assume the risk that they will be able to buy the stock at a more favorable price than the price at which they sold short. [. . .]*
> *To calculate short interest in Nasdaq stocks, NASD member firms are instructed to report to the NASDR TS-Customer Advocacy & Quality Management Department, on a monthly basis, their short positions, for all accounts, in shares, warrants, units, ADRs, and convertible preferreds resulting from short sales. Once the short position reports*

are received by the Product Deployment and Support Department, the short interest is then compiled for each Nasdaq security. [...]

The monthly short interest information does include the adjustment for stock splits. The adjustment to the short interest for stocks that split on or before the reporting settlement date will automatically be reflected in the most current reporting period. However, for stock splits that occur after the settlement date, the adjustment will be reflected in the following reporting period.

You can download a monthly text file listing short interest positions for all Nasdaq issues by going to: http://www.marketdata.nasdaq.com/mr4c.html (link valid as of 05/19/2002). The following is a choice of the short interest of the first five as well as some prominent stocks of their April 2002 listing:

security name	security symbol	current shares short	prev. month shares short	change in shares short	% change in shares short	average daily volume
02Micro International Limited	OIIM	2846753	713442	2133311	299	797977
1-800 Contacts, Inc.	CTAC	3047592	2571988	475604	18	190341
1-800 FLOWERS.COM, Inc.	FLWS	466209	532703	−66494	−12	57857
1-800-ATTORNEY, Inc.	ATTY	733	576	157	27	8646
1st Constitution Bancorp (NJ)	FCCY	132	0	132	0	1099
Intel Corporation	INTC	74613777	80023642	−5409865	−7	42550432
Juniper Networks, Inc.	JNPR	25482068	29421056	−3938988	−13	18507315
Yahoo! Inc.	YHOO	27236052	27338277	−102225	0	9687090
priceline.com Incorporated	PCLN	3748882	4417898	−669016	−15	1842726

In general, stocks that lend themselves to some speculation and stocks around corporate events (mergers and acquisition, dividend dates, etc.) with uncertain outcomes will have a particularly high short interest.

It is theoretically possible to have short interest of more than 100%, because some market participants (e.g., market makers) have the ability to short sell a stock without having a locate, i.e., having someone who actually owns the stock and has agreed to lend it.

Question 1.12.

We are interested in borrowing the asset "money" to buy a house. Therefore, we go to an owner of the asset, called Bank. The Bank provides the dollar amount, say $250,000, in digital form in our mortgage account. As $250,000 is a large amount of money, the bank is subject to substantial **credit risk** (e.g., we may lose our job) and demands a **collateral**. Although the money itself is not subject to large variations in price (besides inflation risk, it is difficult to imagine a reason for money to vary in value), the Bank knows that we want to buy a house, and real estate prices vary substantially. Therefore, the Bank wants more collateral than the $250,000 they are lending.

In fact, as the Bank is only lending up to 80% of the value of the house, we could get a mortgage of $250,000 for a house that is worth $250,000 \div 0.8 = $312,500$. We see that the bank factored in a **haircut** of $312,500 - $250,000 = $62,500$ to protect itself from credit risk and adverse fluctuations in property prices.

We buy back the asset money over a long horizon of time by reducing our mortgage through annuity payments.

Chapter 2
An Introduction to Forwards and Options

Question 2.2.

Since we sold the stock initially, our payoff at expiration from being short the stock is negative.

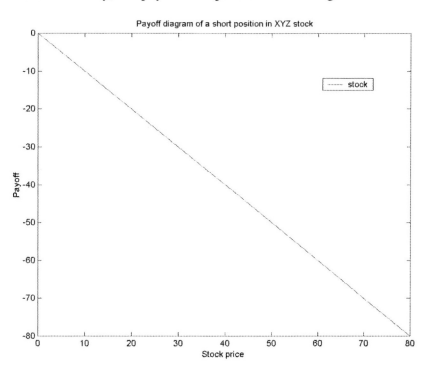

In order to obtain the profit diagram at expiration, we have to lend out the money we received from the short sale of the stock. We do so by buying a bond for $50. After one year we receive from the investment in the bond: $\$50 \times (1 + 0.1) = \$55$. The second figure shows the graph of the sold stock, of the money we receive from the investment in the bond, and of the sum of the two positions, which is the profit graph. The arrows show that at a stock price of $55, the profit at expiration is indeed zero.

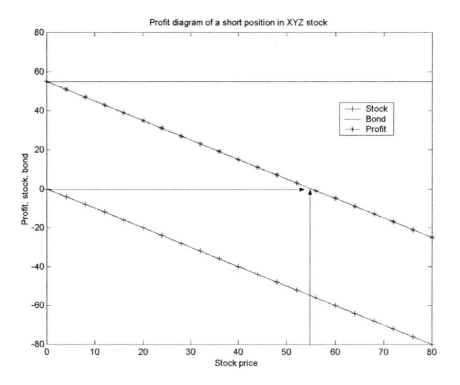

Question 2.4.

a)   The payoff to a long forward at expiration is equal to:

Payoff to long forward $=$ Spot price at expiration − forward price

Therefore, we can construct the following table:

Price of asset in 6 months	Agreed forward price	Payoff to the long forward
40	50	−10
45	50	−5
50	50	0
55	50	5
60	50	10

b)   The payoff to a purchased call option at expiration is:

Payoff to call option $= \max[0,$ spot price at expiration − strike price$]$

The strike is given: It is $50. Therefore, we can construct the following table:

Price of asset in 6 months	Strike price	Payoff to the call option
40	50	0
45	50	0
50	50	0
55	50	5
60	50	10

c)   If we compare the two contracts, we immediately see that the call option has a protection for adverse movements in the price of the asset: If the spot price is below $50, the buyer of the call option can walk away, and need not incur a loss. The buyer of the long forward incurs a loss, while he has the same payoff as the buyer of the call option if the spot price is above $50. Therefore, the call option should be more expensive. It is this attractive option to walk away that we have to pay for.

Question 2.6.

We need to solve the following equation to determine the effective annual interest rate: $91 × (1 + r) = $100. We obtain $r = 0.0989$, which means that the effective annual interest rate is approximately 9.9%.

Remember that when we drew profit diagrams for the forward or call option, we drew the payoff on the vertical axis, and the index price at the expiration of the contract on the horizontal axis. In this case, the particularity is that the default-free zero-coupon bond will pay exactly $100, no matter what the stock price is. Therefore, the payoff diagram is just a horizontal line, intersecting the y-axis at $100.

The textbook provides the answer to the question concerning the profit diagram in the section "Zero-Coupon Bonds in Payoff and Profit Diagrams." When we were calculating profits, we saw that we had to find the future value of the initial investment. In this case, our initial investment is $91. How do we find the future value? We use the current risk-free interest rate and multiply the initial investment by it. However, as our bond is default-free, and does not bear coupons, the effective annual interest rate is exactly the 9.9% we have calculated before. Therefore, the future value of $91 is $91 × (1 + 0.0989) = $100, and our profit in six months is zero!

Question 2.8.

We saw in question 2.7. b) that there is no advantage in buying either the stock or the forward contract if we can borrow to buy a stock today (so both strategies do not require any initial cash) and if the profit from this strategy is the same as the profit of a long forward contract. The profit of a long forward contract with a price for delivery of $53 is equal to: $S_T - $53, where S_T is the (unknown) value of one share of XYZ at expiration of the forward contract in one year. If we borrow $50 today to buy one share of XYZ stock (that costs $50), we have to repay in one year: $50 × (1 + r). Our total profit in one year from borrowing to buy one share of XYZ is therefore:

$\$S_T - \$50 \times (1 + r)$. Now we can equate the two profit equations and solve for the interest rate r:

$$
\begin{aligned}
\$S_T - \$53 &= \$S_T - \$50 \times (1 + r) \\
\Leftrightarrow \quad \$53 &= \$50 \times (1 + r) \\
\Leftrightarrow \quad \frac{\$53}{\$50} - 1 &= r \\
\Leftrightarrow \quad r &= 0.06
\end{aligned}
$$

Therefore, the 1-year effective interest rate that is consistent with no advantage to either buying the stock or forward contract is 6 percent.

Question 2.10.

a)   Figure 2.7 depicts the profit from a long call option on the S&R index with 6 months to expiration and a strike price of $1,000 if the future price of the option premium is $95.68. The profit of the long call option is:

$$
\max[0, S_T - \$1,000] - \$95.68
$$
$$
\Leftrightarrow \quad \max[-\$95.68, S_T - \$1,095.68]
$$

where S_T is the (unknown) value of the S&R index at expiration of the call option in six months. In order to find the S&R index price at which the call option diagram intersects the x-axis, we have to set the above equation equal to zero. We get: $S_T - \$1,095.68 = 0 \Leftrightarrow S_T = \$1,095.68$. This is the only solution, as the other part of the maximum function, $-\$95.68$, is always less than zero.

b)   The profit of the 6 month forward contract with a forward price of $1,020 is: $\$S_T - \$1,020$. In order to find the S&R index price at which the call option and the forward contract have the same profit, we need to set both parts of the maximum function of the profit of the call option equal to the profit of the forward contract and see which part permits a solution. First, we see immediately that $\$S_T - \$1,020 = \$S_T - \$1,095.68$ does not have a solution. But we can solve the other leg: $\$S_T - \$1,020 = -\$95.68 \Leftrightarrow S_T = \$924.32$, which is the value given in the exercise.

Question 2.12.

a)   Long Forward
The maximum loss occurs if the stock price at expiration is zero (the stock price cannot be less than zero, because companies have limited liability). The forward then pays $0 - $ Forward price. The maximum gain is unlimited. The stock price at expiration could theoretically grow to infinity, there is no bound. We make a lot of money if the stock price grows to infinity (or to a very large amount).

b)   Short Forward
The profit for a short forward contract is forward price $-$ stock price at expiration. The maximum loss occurs if the stock price raises sharply, there is no bound to it, so it could grow to infinity. The maximum gain occurs if the stock price is zero.

c)   Long Call

We will not exercise the call option if the stock price at expiration is less than the strike price. Consequently, the only thing we lose is the future value of the premium we paid initially to buy the option. As the stock price can grow very large (and without bound), and our payoff grows linearly in the terminal stock price once it is higher than the strike, there is no limit to our gain.

d)   Short Call

We have no control over the exercise decision when we write a call. The buyer of the call option decides whether to exercise or not, and he will only exercise if he makes a profit. As we have the opposite side, we will never make any money at the expiration of the call option. Our profit is restricted to the future value of the premium, and we make this maximum profit whenever the stock price at expiration is smaller than the strike price. However, the stock price at expiration can be very large and has no bound, and as our loss grows linearly in the terminal stock price, there is no limit to our loss.

e)   Long Put

We will not exercise the put option if the stock price at expiration is larger than the strike price. Consequently, the only thing we lose whenever the terminal stock price is larger than the strike is the future value of the premium we paid initially to buy the option. We will profit from a decline in the stock prices. However, stock prices cannot be smaller than zero, so our maximum gain is restricted to strike price less the future value of the premium and it occurs at a terminal stock price of zero.

f)   Short Put

We have no control over the exercise decision when we write a put. The buyer of the put option decides whether to exercise or not, and he will only exercise if he makes a profit. As we have the opposite side, we will never make any money at the expiration of the put option. Our profit is restricted to the future value of the premium, and we make this maximum profit whenever the stock price at expiration is greater than the strike price. However, we lose money whenever the stock price is smaller than the strike, hence the largest loss occurs when the stock price attains its smallest possible value, zero. We lose the strike price because somebody sells us an asset for the strike that is worth nothing. We are only compensated by the future value of the premium we received.

Question 2.14.

In order to be able to draw profit diagrams, we need to find the future values of the put premia. They are:

a)   35-strike put: $1.53 \times (1 + 0.08) = 1.6524

b)   40-strike put: $3.26 \times (1 + 0.08) = 3.5208

c)   45-strike put: $5.75 \times (1 + 0.08) = 6.21

We get the following payoff diagrams:

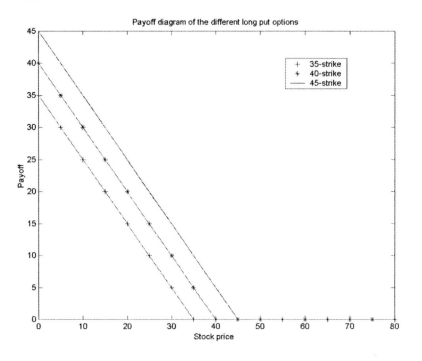

We get the profit diagram by deducting the option premia from the payoff graphs. The profit diagram looks as follows:

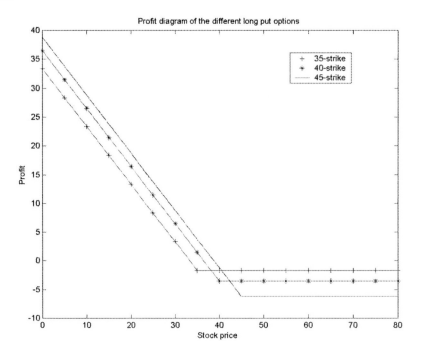

Intuitively, whenever the 35-strike put option pays off (i.e., has a payoff bigger than zero), the 40-strike and the 35-strike options also pay off. However, there are some instances in which the

40-strike option pays off and the 35-strike options does not. Similarly, there are some instances in which the 45-strike option pays off, and neither the 40-strike nor the 35-strike pay off. Therefore, the 45-strike offers more potential than the 40- and 35-strike, and the 40-strike offers more potential than the 35-strike. We pay for these additional payoff possibilities by initially paying a higher premium. It makes sense that the premium is increasing in the strike price.

Question 2.16.

The following is a copy of an Excel spreadsheet that solves the problem:

Chapter 3
Insurance, Collars, and Other Strategies

Question 3.2.

This question constructs a position that is the opposite to the position of Table 3.1. Therefore, we should get the exact opposite results from Table 3.1. and the associated figures. Mimicking Table 3.1., we indeed have:

S&R Index	S&R Put	Payoff	−(Cost + Interest)	Profit
−900.00	−100.00	−1000.00	1095.68	95.68
−950.00	−50.00	−1000.00	1095.68	95.68
−1000.00	0.00	−1000.00	1095.68	95.68
−1050.00	0.00	−1050.00	1095.68	45.68
−1100.00	0.00	−1100.00	1095.68	−4.32
−1150.00	0.00	−1150.00	1095.68	−54.32
−1200.00	0.00	−1200.00	1095.68	−104.32

On the next page, we see the corresponding payoff and profit diagrams. Please note that they match the combined payoff and profit diagrams of Figure 3.5. Only the axes have different scales.

Payoff-diagram:

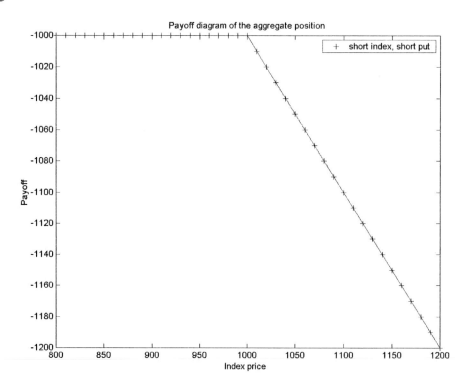

Profit diagram:

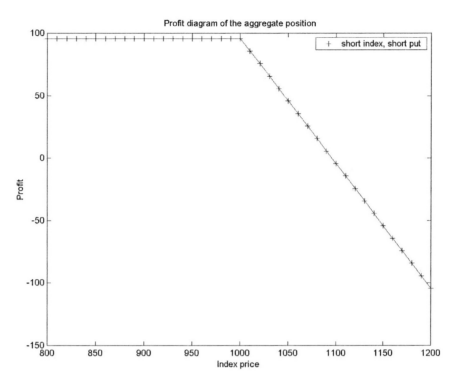

Question 3.4.

This question is another application of Put-Call-Parity. Initially, we have the following cost to enter into the combined position: We receive $1,000 from the short sale of the index, and we have to pay the call premium. Therefore, the future value of our cost is: $\left(\$120.405 - \$1,000\right) \times (1 + 0.02) = -\$897.19$. Note that a negative cost means that we initially have an inflow of money.

Now, we can directly proceed to draw the payoff diagram:

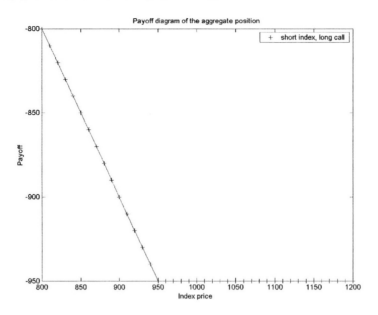

We can clearly see from the figure that the payoff graph of the short index and the long call looks like a fixed obligation of $950, which is alleviated by a long put position with a strike price of 950. The following profit diagram, including the cost for the combined position, confirms this:

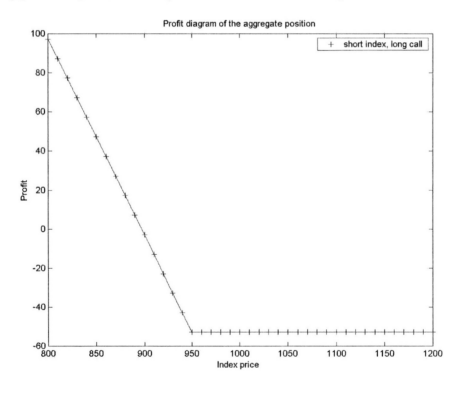

Question 3.6.

We now move from a graphical representation and verification of the Put-Call-Parity to a mathematical representation. Let us first consider the payoff of (a). If we buy the index (let us name it S), we receive at the time of expiration T of the options simply S_T.

The payoffs of part (b) are a little bit more complicated. If we deal with options and the maximum function, it is convenient to split the future values of the index into two regions: one where $S_T < K$ and another one where $S_T \geq K$. We then look at each region separately, and hope to be able to draw a conclusion when we look at the aggregate position.

We have for the payoffs in (b):

Instrument	$S_T < K = 950$	$S_T \geq K = 950$
Get repayment of loan	$931.37 \times 1.02 = 950$	$931.37 \times 1.02 = 950$
Long Call Option	$\max(S_T - 950, 0) = 0$	$S_T - 950$
Short Put Option	$-\max(\$950 - S_T, 0)$ $= S_T - \$950$	0
Total	S_T	S_T

We now see that the total aggregate position only gives us S_T, no matter what the final index value is—but this is the same payoff as in part (a). Our proof for the payoff equivalence is complete.

Now let us turn to the profits. If we buy the index today, we need to finance it. Therefore, we borrow $1,000, and have to repay $1,020 after one year. The profit for part (a) is thus: $S_T - \$1,020$.

The profits of the aggregate position in part (b) are the payoffs, less the future value of the call premium plus the future value of the put premium (because we have sold the put), and less the future value of the loan we gave initially. Note that we already know that a risk-less bond is canceling out of the profit calculations. We can again tabulate:

Instrument	$S_T < K$	$S_T \geq K$
Get repayment of loan	$931.37 \times 1.02 = \$950$	$931.37 \times 1.02 = \$950$
Future value of given loan	$-\$950$	$-\$950$
Long Call Option	$\max(S_T - 950, 0) = 0$	$S_T - 950$
Future value call premium	$-\$120.405 \times 1.02 = -\$122.81$	$-\$120.405 \times 1.02 = -\$122.81$
Short Put Option	$-\max(\$950 - S_T, 0)$ $= S_T - \$950$	0
Future value put premium	$\$51.777 \times 1.02 = \$52.81$	$\$51.777 \times 1.02 = \$52.81$
Total	$S_T - 1020$	$S_T - 1020$

Indeed, we see that the profits for part (a) and part (b) are identical as well.

Question 3.8.

This question is a direct application of the Put-Call-Parity. We will use equation (3.1) in the following, and input the given variables:

$$Call\,(K,t) - Put\,(K,t) = PV\left(F_{0,t} - K\right)$$
$$\Leftrightarrow \quad Call\,(K,t) - Put\,(K,t) - PV\left(F_{0,t}\right) = -PV\,(K)$$
$$\Leftrightarrow \quad Call\,(K,t) - Put\,(K,t) - S_0 = -PV\,(K)$$
$$\Leftrightarrow \quad \$109.20 - \$60.18 - \$1{,}000 = -\frac{K}{1.02}$$
$$\Leftrightarrow \quad K = \$970.00$$

Question 3.10.

The strategy of selling a call (or put) and buying a call (or put) at a higher strike is called call (put) bear spread. In order to draw the profit diagrams, we need to find the future value of the cost of entering in the bull spread positions. We have:

Cost of call bear spread: $\left(\$71.802 - \$120.405\right) \times 1.02 = -\$49.575$
Cost of put bear spread: $\left(\$101.214 - \$51.777\right) \times 1.02 = \$50.426$

The payoff diagram shows that the payoff to the call bear spread is uniformly less than the payoffs to the put bear spread. The difference is exactly \$100, equal to the difference in strikes and as well equal to the difference in the future value of the costs of the spreads.

There is a difference, because the call bear spread has a negative initial cost, i.e., we are receiving money if we enter into it.

The higher initial cost for the put bear spread is exactly offset by the higher payoff so that the profits of both strategies turn out to be the same. It is easy to show this with equation (3.1), the put-call-parity.

Payoff-Diagram:

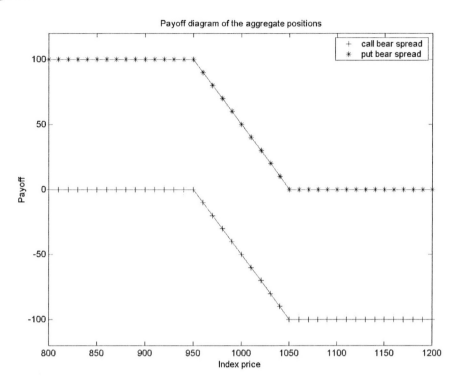

Profit Diagram:

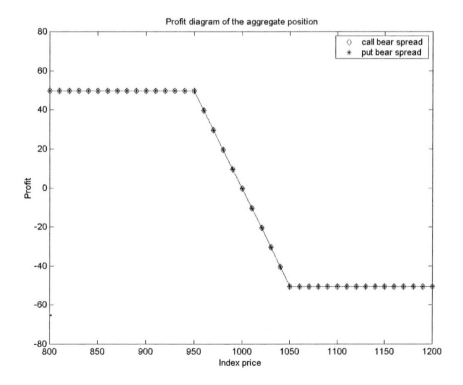

Question 3.12.

Our initial cash required to put on the collar, i.e. the net option premium, is as follows: $-\$51.873 + \$51.777 = -\$0.096$. Therefore, we receive only 10 cents if we enter into this collar. The position is very close to a zero-cost collar.

The profit diagram looks as follows:

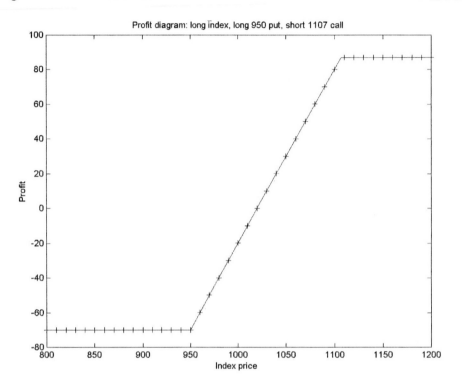

If we compare this profit diagram with the profit diagram of the previous exercise (3.11.), we see that we traded in the additional call premium (that limited our losses after index decreases) against more participation on the upside. Please note that both maximum loss and gain are higher than in question 3.11.

Question 3.14.

a)   This question deals with the option trading strategy known as Box spread. We saw earlier that if we deal with options and the maximum function, it is convenient to split the future values of the index into different regions. Let us name the final value of the S&R index S_T. We have two strike prices, therefore we will use three regions: One in which $S_T < 950$, one in which $950 \le S_T < 1,000$ and another one in which $S_T \ge 1,000$. We then look at each region separately, and hope to be able to see that indeed when we aggregate, there is no S&R risk when we look at the aggregate position.

Instrument	$S_T < 950$	$950 \leq S_T < 1,000$	$S_T \geq 1,000$
long 950 call	0	$S_T - \$950$	$S_T - \$950$
short 1000 call	0	0	$\$1,000 - S_T$
short 950 put	$S_T - \$950$	0	0
long 1000 put	$\$1,000 - S_T$	$\$1,000 - S_T$	0
Total	$\$50$	$\$50$	$\$50$

We see that there is no occurrence of the final index value in the row labeled total. The option position does not contain S&R price risk.

b)   The initial cost is the sum of the long option premia less the premia we receive for the sold options. We have:

Cost $\$120.405 - \$93.809 - \$51.77 + \$74.201 = \$49.027$

c)   The payoff of the position after 6 months is $50, as we can see from the above table.

d)   The implicit interest rate of the cash flows is: $\$50.00 \div \$49.027 = 1.019 \cong 1.02$. The implicit interest rate is indeed 2 percent.

Question 3.16.

A bull spread or a bear spread can never have an initial premium of zero, because we are buying the same number of calls (or puts) that we are selling and the two legs of the bull and bear spreads have different strikes. A zero initial premium would mean that two calls (or puts) with different strikes have the same price—and we know by now that two instruments that have different payoff structures and the same underlying risk cannot have the same price without creating an arbitrage opportunity.

A symmetric butterfly spread cannot have a premium of zero because it would violate the convexity condition of options.

Question 3.18.

The following three figures show the individual legs of each of the three suggested strategies. The last subplot shows the aggregate position. It is evident from the figures that you can indeed use all the suggested strategies to construct the same butterfly spread. Another method to show the claim of 3.18. mathematically would be to establish the equivalence by using the Put-Call-Parity on b) and c) and showing that you can write it in terms of the instruments of a).

profit diagram part a)

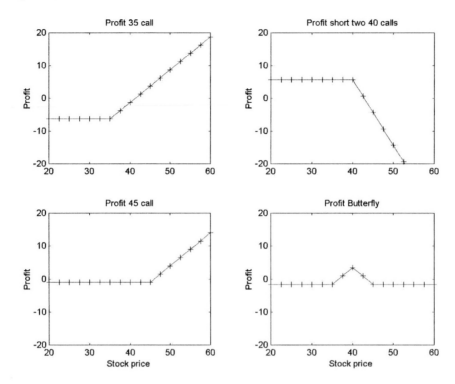

profit diagram part b)

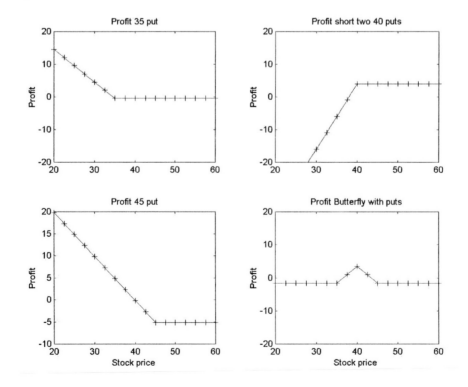

profit diagram part c)

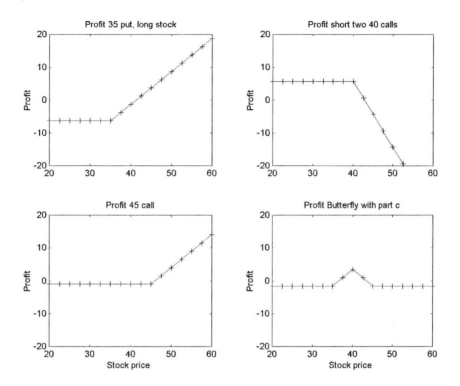

Question 3.20.

Use separate cells for the strike price and the quantities you buy and sell for each strike (i.e., make use of the plus or minus sign). Then, use the maximum function to calculate payoffs and profits.

The best way to solve this problem is probably to have the calculations necessary for the payoff and profit diagrams run in the background, e.g., in another auxiliary table that you are referencing to. Define the boundaries for the calculations dynamically and symmetrically around the current stock price. Then use the diagram function with the line style to draw the diagrams.

Chapter 4
Introduction to Risk Management

Question 4.2.

If the forward price were $0.80 instead of $1, we would get the following table:

Copper price in one year	Total cost	Unhedged profit	Profit on short forward	Net income on hedged profit
$0.70	$0.90	−$0.20	$0.10	−$0.10
$0.80	$0.90	−$0.10	$0	−$0.10
$0.90	$0.90	0	−$0.10	−$0.10
$1.00	$0.90	$0.10	−$0.20	−$0.10
$1.10	$0.90	$0.20	−$0.30	−$0.10
$1.20	$0.90	$0.30	−$0.40	−$0.10

With a forward price of $0.45, we have:

Copper price in one year	Total cost	Unhedged profit	Profit on short forward	Net income on hedged profit
$0.70	$0.90	−$0.20	−$0.25	−$0.45
$0.80	$0.90	−$0.10	−$0.35	−$0.45
$0.90	$0.90	0	−$0.45	−$0.45
$1.00	$0.90	$0.10	−$0.55	−$0.45
$1.10	$0.90	$0.20	−$0.65	−$0.45
$1.20	$0.90	$0.30	−$0.75	−$0.45

Although the copper forward price of $0.45 is below our total costs of $0.90, it is higher than the variable cost of $0.40. It still makes sense to produce copper, because even at a price of $0.45 in one year, we will be able to partially cover our fixed costs.

Question 4.4.

We will explicitly calculate the profit for the $1.00-strike and show figures for all three strikes. The future value of the $1.00-strike call premium amounts to: $0.0376 \times 1.062 = 0.04.

Copper price in one year	Total cost	Unhedged profit	Profit on short $1.00-strike call option	Call premium received	Net income on hedged profit
$0.70	$0.90	−$0.20	0	$0.04	−$0.16
$0.80	$0.90	−$0.10	0	$0.04	−$0.06
$0.90	$0.90	0	0	$0.04	$0.04
$1.00	$0.90	$0.10	0	$0.04	$0.14
$1.10	$0.90	$0.20	−$0.10	$0.04	$0.14
$1.20	$0.90	$0.30	−$0.20	$0.04	$0.14

We obtain the following payoff graphs:

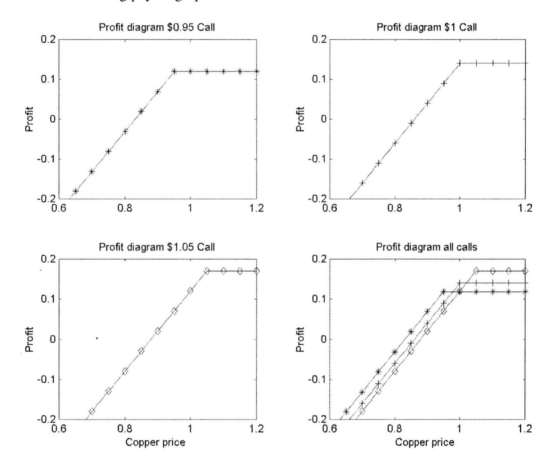

Question 4.6.

a)

Copper price in one year	Total cost	Profit on short 1.025 put	Profit on two long $0.975 puts	Net premium	Hedged profit
$0.70	$0.90	−$0.325	$0.55	$0.0022	$0.0228
$0.80	$0.90	−$0.225	$0.35	$0.0022	$0.0228
$0.90	$0.90	−$0.125	$0.150	$0.0022	$0.0228
$1.00	$0.90	−$0.025	0	$0.0022	$0.0728
$1.10	$0.90	0	0	$0.0022	$0.1978
$1.20	$0.90	0	0	$0.0022	$0.2978

We can see from the following profit diagram (and the above table) that in the case of a favorable increase in copper prices, the hedged profit is almost identical to the unhedged profit.

Profit diagram:

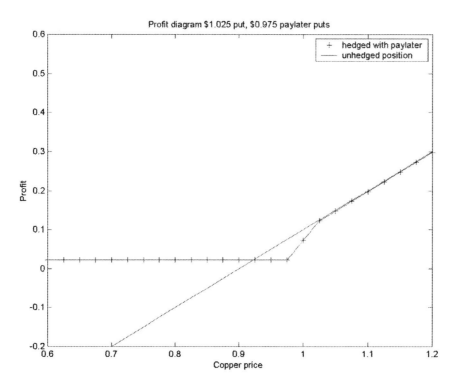

b)

Copper price in one year	Total cost	Profit on two short 1.034 put	Profit on three long $1 puts	Net premium	Hedged profit
$0.70	$0.90	−$0.6680	$0.9	$0.0002	$0.0318
$0.80	$0.90	−$0.4680	$0.6	$0.0002	$0.0318
$0.90	$0.90	−$0.2680	$0.3	$0.0002	$0.0318
$1.00	$0.90	−$0.0680	0	$0.0002	$0.0318
$1.10	$0.90	0	0	$0.0002	$0.1998
$1.20	$0.90	0	0	$0.0002	$0.2998

We can see from the following profit diagram (and the above table) that in the case of a favorable increase in copper prices, the hedged profit is almost identical to the unhedged profit.

Profit diagram:

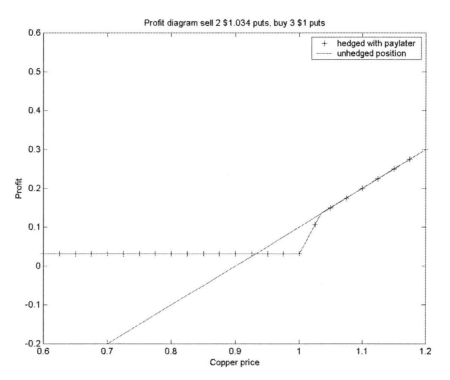

Question 4.8.

In this exercise, we need to first find the future value of the call premia. For the $1-strike call, it is: $0.0376 × 1.062 = $0.04. The following table shows the profit calculations of the $1.00-strike call. The calculations for the two other calls are exactly similar. The figures on the next page compare the profit diagrams of all three possible hedging strategies.

Copper price in one year	Total cost	Unhedged profit	Profit on long $1.00-strike call	Call premium	Net income on hedged profit
$0.70	$5.70	$0.50	0	$0.04	$0.46
$0.80	$5.80	$0.40	0	$0.04	$0.36
$0.90	$5.90	$0.30	0	$0.04	$0.26
$1.00	$6.00	$0.20	0	$0.04	$0.16
$1.10	$6.10	$0.10	$0.10	$0.04	$0.16
$1.20	$6.20	0	$0.20	$0.04	$0.16

We obtain the following profit diagrams:

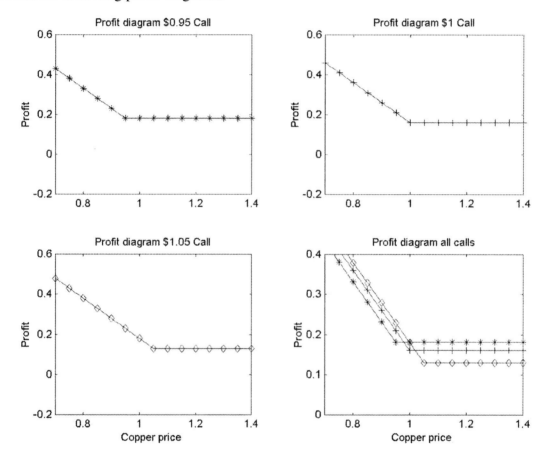

Question 4.10.

Telco will sell collars, which means that they buy the call leg and sell the put leg. We have to compute for each case the net option premium position, and find its future value. We have for:

a) $\left(\$0.0376 - \$0.0178\right) \times 1.062 = \$0.021$

b) $\left(\$0.0274 - \$0.0265\right) \times 1.062 = \$0.001$

c) $\left(\$0.0649 - \$0.0178\right) \times 1.062 = \$0.050$

a)

Copper price in one year	Total cost	Unhedged profit	Profit on short .95 put	Profit on long $1.00 call	Net premium	Hedged profit
$0.70	$5.70	$0.50	−$0.25	0	$0.021	$0.2290
$0.80	$5.80	$0.40	−$0.15	0	$0.021	$0.2290
$0.90	$5.90	$0.30	−$0.05	0	$0.021	$0.2290
$1.00	$6.00	$0.20	$0	0	$0.021	$0.1790
$1.10	$6.10	$0.10	0	$0.10	$0.021	$0.1790
$1.20	$6.20	0	0	$0.20	$0.021	$0.1790

Profit diagram:

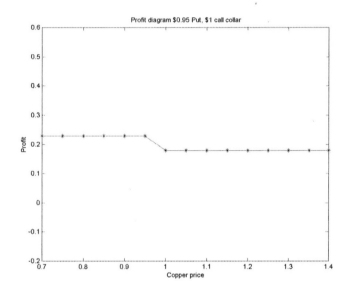

b)

Copper price in one year	Total cost	Unhedged profit	Profit on short .95 put	Profit on long $1.025 call	Net premium	Hedged profit
$0.70	$5.70	$0.50	−$0.275	0	$0.001	$0.2240
$0.80	$5.80	$0.40	−$0.175	0	$0.001	$0.2240
$0.90	$5.90	$0.30	−$0.075	0	$0.001	$0.2240
$1.00	$6.00	$0.20	$0	0	$0.001	$0.1990
$1.10	$6.10	$0.10	0	$0.0750	$0.001	$0.1740
$1.20	$6.20	0	0	$0.1750	$0.001	$0.1740

Profit diagram:

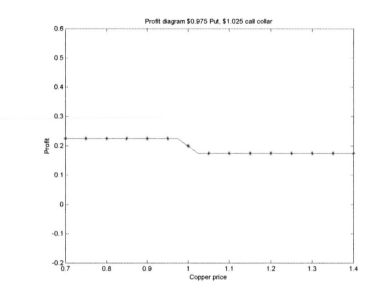

c)

Copper price in one year	Total cost	Unhedged profit	Profit on short .95 put	Profit on long $.95 call	Net premium	Hedged profit
$0.70	$5.70	$0.50	−$0.25	0	$0.05	$0.2
$0.80	$5.80	$0.40	−$0.15	0	$0.05	$0.2
$0.90	$5.90	$0.30	−$0.05	0	$0.05	$0.2
$1.00	$6.00	$0.20	0	$0.050	$0.05	$0.2
$1.10	$6.10	$0.10	0	$0.150	$0.05	$0.2
$1.20	$6.20	0	0	$0.250	$0.05	$0.2

We see that we are completely and perfectly hedged. Buying a collar where the put and call leg have equal strike prices perfectly offsets the copper price risk.

Profit diagram:

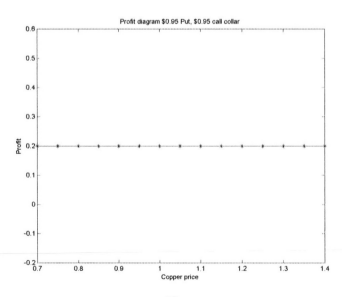

Question 4.12.

This is a very important exercise to really understand the benefits and pitfalls of hedging strategies. Wirco needs copper as an input, which means that its costs increase with the price of copper. We may therefore think that they need to hedge against increases in the copper price. However, we must not forget that the price of wire, the source of Wirco's revenues, also depends positively on the price of copper: the price Wirco can obtain for one unit of wire is $50 plus the price of copper. We will see that those copper price risks cancel each other out. Mathematically,

$$\text{Wirco's cost per unit of wire:} \quad \$3 + \$1.50 + S_T$$
$$\text{Wirco's revenue per unit of wire:} \quad \$5 + S_T$$

and S_T is the price of copper after one year. Therefore, we can determine Wirco's profits as:

$$\text{Profit } = \text{ Revenue} - \text{Cost } = \$5 + S_T - \left(\$3 + \$1.50 + S_T\right) = \$0.50$$

We see that the profits of Wirco do not depend on the price of copper. Cost and revenue copper price risk cancel each other out. If we buy in this situation a long forward contract, we do in fact introduce copper price risk! To understand this, add a long forward contract to the profit equation:

$$\text{Profit with forward: } = \$5 + S_T - \left(\$3 + \$1.50 + S_T\right) + S_T - \$1 = S_T - \$0.50$$

To summarize,

Copper price in one year	Total cost	Total revenue	Unhedged profit	Profit on long forward	Net income on 'hedged' profit
$0.70	$5.20	$5.70	$0.50	−$0.30	$0.20
$0.80	$5.30	$5.80	$0.50	−$0.20	$0.30
$0.90	$5.40	$5.90	$0.50	−$0.10	$0.40
$1.00	$5.50	$6.00	$0.50	0	$0.50
$1.10	$5.60	$6.10	$0.50	$0.10	$0.60
$1.20	$5.70	$6.20	$0.50	$0.20	$0.70

Question 4.14.

Hedging should never be thought of as a profit increasing action. A company that hedges merely shifts profits from good to bad states of the relevant price risk that the hedge seeks to diminish.

The value of the reduced profits, should the gold price rise, subsidizes the payment to Golddiggers should the gold price fall. Therefore, a company may use a hedge for one of the reasons stated in the textbook; however, it is not correct to compare hedged and unhedged companies from an accounting perspective.

Question 4.16.

a) Expected pre-tax profit

Firm A: $E[\text{Profit}] = 0.5 \times (\$1,000) + 0.5 \times (-\$600) = \$200$
Firm B: $E[\text{Profit}] = 0.5 \times (\$300) + 0.5 \times (\$100) = \$200$

Both firms have the same pre-tax profit.

b) Expected after tax profit.

Firm A:

		bad state	good state
(1)	Pre-Tax Operating Income	−$600	$1,000
(2)	Taxable Income	$0	$ 1,000
(3)	Tax @ 40%	0	$400
(3b)	Tax Credit	$240	0
	After-Tax Income (including Tax credit)	−$360	$600

This gives an expected after-tax profit for firm A of:

$$E[\text{Profit}] = 0.5 \times (-\$360) + 0.5 \times (\$600) = \$120$$

Firm B:

		bad state	good state
(1)	Pre-Tax Operating Income	$100	$300
(2)	Taxable Income	$100	$300
(3)	Tax @ 40%	$40	$120
(3b)	Tax Credit	0	0
	After-Tax Income (including Tax credit)	$60	$180

This gives an expected after-tax profit for firm B of:

$$E[\text{Profit}] = 0.5 \times (\$60) + 0.5 \times (\$180) = \$120$$

If losses receive full credit for tax losses, the tax code does not have an effect on the expected after-tax profits of firms that have the same expected pre-tax profits, but different cash-flow variability.

Question 4.18.

Auric Enterprises is using gold as an input. Therefore, it would like to hedge against price increases in gold.

a) The cost of this collar today is the premium of the purchased 440-strike call ($2.49) less the premium for the sold 400-strike put. We calculate a cost of $2.49 − $2.21 = −$0.28, which means that Auric in fact generates a revenue from entering into this collar.

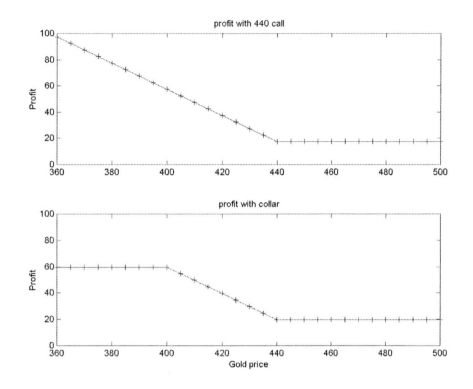

b)   A good starting point are the values of part a). You see that both put and call are worth approximately the same, therefore start shrinking the 440 – 400 span symmetrically until you get a difference of 30, and then do some trial and error. This should bring you the following values:

The call strike is 435.52, and the put strike is 405.52. Both call and put have a premium of $3.425.

Question 4.20.

a)   Since we know that the value of a call is decreasing in the strike, and we need to sell two call options, the Black-Scholes prices of which equal the 440-strike call price, we know that we have to look for a higher strike price. Trial and error results in a strike price of 448.93. The premium of the 440-strike call is $2.4944, and indeed the Black-Scholes premium of the 448.93 strike call is $1.2472.

b)   Profit diagram:

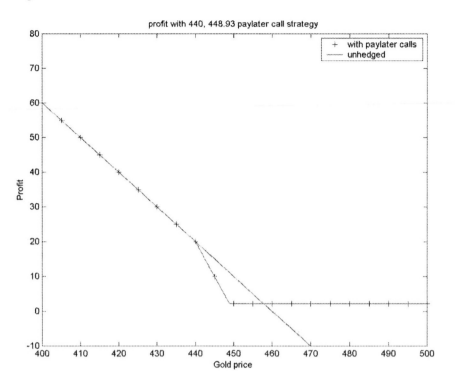

Question 4.22.

a)   We have the following table:

Price	Quantity	Revenue
3	1.5	4.5
3	0.8	2.4
2	1	2
2	0.6	1.2

Using Excel's function STDEVP(4.5,2.4,2,1.2), we obtain a value of 1.2194 for the standard deviation of total revenue for Scenario C.

b)   Using any standard software's command (or doing it by hand!) to determine the correlation coefficient, we obtain a value of 0.7586.

Question 4.24.

a)   The expected quantity of production is $0.25 \times (1.5 + 0.8 + 1 + 0.6) = 0.975$ million bushels of corn.

b)

Price	Quantity	Unhedged revenue	Futures gain from shorting 0.975m contracts	Total
3	1.5m	4.5m	$-0.5 \times 0.975m$ $= -0.4875m$	4.0125m
3	0.8m	2.4m	$-0.5 \times 0.975m$ $= -0.4875m$	1.9125m
2	1m	2m	$0.5 \times 0.975m$ $= 0.4875m$	2.4875m
2	0.6m	1.2m	$0.5 \times 0.975m$ $= 0.4875m$	1.6875m

Using Excel's function STDEVP(4.0125, 1.9125, 2.4875, 1.6875), we obtain a value of 0.907004 for the standard deviation of the optimally hedged revenue for Scenario C. We see that we were able to reduce the variance of our revenues, albeit to a lesser degree than with the optimally hedged portfolio.

Chapter 5
Financial Forwards and Futures

Question 5.2.

a)   The owner of the stock is entitled to receive dividends. As we will get the stock only in one year, the value of the prepaid forward contract is today's stock price, less the present value of the four dividend payments:

$$F_{0,T}^P = \$50 - \sum_{i=1}^{4} \$1 e^{-0.06 \times \frac{3}{12}i} = \$50 - \$0.985 - \$0.970 - \$0.956 - \$0.942$$

$$= \$50 - \$3.853 = \$46.147$$

b)   The forward price is equivalent to the future value of the prepaid forward. With an interest rate of 6 percent and an expiration of the forward in one year, we thus have:

$$F_{0,T} = F_{0,T}^P \times e^{0.06 \times 1} = \$46.147 \times e^{0.06 \times 1} = \$46.147 \times 1.0618 = \$49.00$$

Question 5.4.

This question asks us to familiarize ourselves with the forward valuation equation.

a)   We plug the continuously compounded interest rate and the time to expiration in years into the valuation formula and notice that the time to expiration is 6 months, or 0.5 years. We have:

$$F_{0,T} = S_0 \times e^{r \times T} = \$35 \times e^{0.05 \times 0.5} = \$35 \times 1.0253 = \$35.886$$

b)   The annualized forward premium is calculated as:

$$\text{annualized forward premium} = \frac{1}{T} \ln \left(\frac{F_{0,T}}{S_0} \right) = \frac{1}{0.5} \ln \left(\frac{\$35.50}{\$35} \right) = 0.0284$$

c)   For the case of continuous dividends, the forward premium is simply the difference between the risk-free rate and the dividend yield:

$$\text{annualized forward premium} = \frac{1}{T} \ln \left(\frac{F_{0,T}}{S_0} \right) = \frac{1}{T} \ln \left(\frac{S_0 \times e^{(r-\delta)T}}{S_0} \right)$$

$$= \frac{1}{T} \ln \left(e^{(r-\delta)T} \right) = \frac{1}{T} (r - \delta) T$$

$$= r - \delta$$

Therefore, we can solve:

$$0.0284 = 0.05 - \delta$$
$$\Leftrightarrow \quad \delta \quad = 0.0216$$

The annualized dividend yield is 2.16 percent.

Question 5.6.

a)   We plug the continuously compounded interest rate, the dividend yield and the time to expiration in years into the valuation formula and notice that the time to expiration is 9 months, or 0.75 years. We have:

$$F_{0,T} = S_0 \times e^{(r-\delta) \times T} = \$1,100 \times e^{(0.05-0.015) \times 0.75} = \$1,100 \times 1.0266 = \$1,129.26$$

b)   We engage in a reverse cash and carry strategy. In particular, we do the following:

Description	Today	In 9 months
Long forward, resulting from customer purchase	0	$S_T - F_{0,T}$
Sell short tailed position of the index	$+S_0 e^{-\delta T}$	$-S_T$
Lend $S_0 e^{-\delta T}$	$-S_0 e^{-\delta T}$	$S_0 \times e^{(r-\delta)T}$
TOTAL	0	$S_0 \times e^{(r-\delta)T} - F_{0,T}$

Specifically, we have:

Description	Today	In 9 months
Long forward, resulting from customer purchase	0	$S_T - \$1,129.26$
Sell short tailed position of the index	$\$1,100 \times .9888$ = 1087.69	$-S_T$
Lend $1,087.69	$-\$1,087.69$	$\$1,087.69 \times e^{0.05 \times 0.75}$ = $\$1,129.26$
TOTAL	0	0

Therefore, the market maker is perfectly hedged. He does not have any risk in the future, because he has successfully created a synthetic short position in the forward contract.

c)

Description	Today	In 9 months
Short forward, resulting from customer purchase	0	$F_{0,T} - S_T$
Buy tailed position in index	$-S_0 e^{-\delta T}$	S_T
Borrow $S_0 e^{-\delta T}$	$S_0 e^{-\delta T}$	$-S_0 \times e^{(r-\delta)T}$
TOTAL	0	$F_{0,T} - S_0 \times e^{(r-\delta)T}$

Specifically, we have:

Description	Today	In 9 months
Short forward, resulting from customer purchase	0	$\$1,129.26 - S_T$
Buy tailed position in index	$-\$1,100 \times .9888$ $= -\$1,087.69$	S_T
Borrow $ 1,087.69	$\$1,087.69$	$-\$1,087.69 \times e^{0.05 \times 0.75}$ $= -\$1,129.26$
TOTAL	0	0

Again, the market maker is perfectly hedged. He does not have any index price risk in the future, because he has successfully created a synthetic long position in the forward contract that perfectly offsets his obligation from the sold forward contract.

Question 5.8.

First, we need to find the fair value of the forward price. We plug the continuously compounded interest rate, the dividend yield and the time to expiration in years into the valuation formula and notice that the time to expiration is 6 months, or 0.5 years. We have:

$$F_{0,T} = S_0 \times e^{(r-\delta) \times T} = \$1,100 \times e^{(0.05-0.02) \times 0.5} = \$1,100 \times 1.01511 = \$1,116.62$$

a)   If we observe a forward price of 1,120, we know that the forward is too expensive, relative to the fair value we have determined. Therefore, we will sell the forward at 1,120, and create a synthetic forward for 1,116.82, making a sure profit of $3.38. As we sell the real forward, we engage in cash and carry arbitrage:

Description	Today	In 9 months
Short forward	0	$\$1,120.00 - S_T$
Buy tailed position in index	$-\$1,100 \times .99$ $= -\$1,089.055$	S_T
Borrow $1,089.055	$\$1,089.055$	$-\$1,116.62$
TOTAL	0	$3.38

This position requires no initial investment, has no index price risk, and has a strictly positive payoff. We have exploited the mispricing with a pure arbitrage strategy.

b)   If we observe a forward price of 1,110, we know that the forward is too cheap, relative to the fair value we have determined. Therefore, we will buy the forward at 1,110, and create a synthetic short forward for 1116.62, thus making a sure profit of $6.62. As we buy the real forward, we engage in a reverse cash and carry arbitrage:

Description	Today	In 9 months
Long forward	0	$S_T - \$1,110.00$
Sell short tailed position in index	$\$1,100 \times .99$ $= \$1,089.055$	$-S_T$
Lend $1,089.055	$-\$1,089.055$	$\$1,116.62$
TOTAL	0	$\$6.62$

This position requires no initial investment, has no index price risk, and has a strictly positive payoff. We have exploited the mispricing with a pure arbitrage strategy.

Question 5.10.

a)   We plug the continuously compounded interest rate, the forward price, the initial index level and the time to expiration in years into the valuation formula and solve for the dividend yield:

$$F_{0,T} = S_0 \times e^{(r-\delta) \times T}$$

$$\Leftrightarrow \quad \frac{F_{0,T}}{S_0} = e^{(r-\delta) \times T}$$

$$\Leftrightarrow \quad \ln\left(\frac{F_{0,T}}{S_0}\right) = (r - \delta) \times T$$

$$\Leftrightarrow \quad \delta = r - \frac{1}{T} \ln\left(\frac{F_{0,T}}{S_0}\right)$$

$$\Rightarrow \quad \delta = 0.05 - \frac{1}{0.75} \ln\left(\frac{1129.257}{1100}\right) = 0.05 - 0.035 = 0.015$$

Remark: Note that this result is consistent with exercise 5.6., in which we had the same forward prices, time to expiration etc.

b)   With a dividend yield of only 0.005, the fair forward price would be:

$$F_{0,T} = S_0 \times e^{(r-\delta) \times T} = 1,100 \times e^{(0.05-0.005) \times 0.75} = 1,100 \times 1.0343 = 1,137.759$$

Therefore, if we think the dividend yield is 0.005, we consider the observed forward price of 1,129.257 to be too cheap. We will therefore buy the forward and create a synthetic short forward, capturing a certain amount of $8.502. We engage in a reverse cash and carry arbitrage:

Description	Today	In 9 months
Long forward	0	$S_T - \$1,129.257$
Sell short tailed position in index	$\$1,100 \times .99626$ $= \$1,095.88$	$-S_T$
Lend $1,095.88	$-\$1,095.88$	$\$1,137.759$
TOTAL	0	$\$8.502$

c)   With a dividend yield of 0.03, the fair forward price would be:

$$F_{0,T} = S_0 \times e^{(r-\delta)\times T} = 1,100 \times e^{(0.05-0.03)\times 0.75} = 1,100 \times 1.01511 = 1,116.62$$

Therefore, if we think the dividend yield is 0.03, we consider the observed forward price of 1,129.257 to be too expensive. We will therefore sell the forward and create a synthetic long forward, capturing a certain amount of $12.637. We engage in a cash and carry arbitrage:

Description	Today	In 9 months
Short forward	0	$\$1,129.257 - S_T$
Buy tailed position in index	$-\$1,100 \times .97775$ $= -\$1,075.526$	S_T
Borrow $1,075.526	$\$1,075.526$	$\$1,116.62$
TOTAL	0	$\$12.637$

Question 5.12.

a)   The notional value of 10 contracts is $10 \times \$250 \times 950 = \$2,375,000$, because each index point is worth $250, we buy 10 contracts and the S&P 500 index level is 950.

With an initial margin of 10% of the notional value, this results in an initial dollar margin of $\$2,375,000 \times 0.10 = \$237,500$.

b)   We first obtain an approximation. Because we have a 10% initial margin, a 2% decline in the futures price will result in a 20% decline in margin. As we will receive a margin call after a 20% decline in the initial margin, the smallest futures price that avoids the maintenance margin call is $950 \times .98 = 931$. However, this calculation ignores the interest that we are able to earn in our margin account.

Let us now calculate the details. We have the right to earn interest on our initial margin position. As the continuously compounded interest rate is currently 6%, after one week, our initial margin has grown to:

$$\$237,500 e^{0.06 \times \frac{1}{52}} = \$237,774.20$$

We will get a margin call if the initial margin falls by 20%. We calculate 80% of the initial margin as:

$$\$237,500 \times 0.8 = \$190,000$$

10 long S&P 500 futures contracts obligate us to pay $2,500 times the forward price at expiration of the futures contract.

Therefore, we have to solve the following equation:

$$\$237,774.20 + (F_{1W} - 950) \times \$2,500 \geq \$190,000$$
$$\Leftrightarrow \quad \$47774.20 \qquad\qquad \geq -(F_{1W} - 950) \times \$2,500$$
$$\Leftrightarrow \quad 19.10968 - 950 \qquad \geq -F_{1W}$$
$$\Leftrightarrow \quad F_{1W} \qquad\qquad \geq 930.89$$

Therefore, the greatest S&P 500 index futures price at which we will receive a margin call is 930.88.

Question 5.14.

An arbitrageur believing that the observed forward price, F(0,T), is too low will undertake a reverse cash and carry arbitrage: Buy the forward, short sell the stock and lend out the proceeds from the short sale. The relevant prices are therefore the bid price of the stock and the lending interest rate. Also, she will incur the transaction costs twice. We have:

Description	Today	In 9 months	
Long forward	0	$S_T - F_{0,T}$	
Sell short tailed position of the index	$+S_0^b e^{-\delta T}$	$-S_T$	
Pay twice transaction cost	$-2 \times k$		
Lend $S_0^b e^{-\delta T} - 2 \times k$	$-S_0^b e^{-\delta T} + 2 \times k$	$\left(+S_0^b e^{-\delta T} - 2 \times k\right) \times e^{r^l T}$	
TOTAL	0	$\left(+S_0^b e^{-\delta T} - 2 \times k\right) \times e^{r^l T} - F_{0,T}$	

To avoid arbitrage, we must have $\left(S_0^b - 2 \times k\right) \times e^{r^l T} - F_{0,T} \leq 0$. This is equivalent to $F_{0,T} \geq \left(S_0^b - 2 \times k\right) \times e^{r^l T}$. Therefore, for any $F_{0,T}$ smaller than this bound, there exist arbitrage opportunities.

Question 5.16.

a)   The one-year futures price is determined as:

$$F_{0,1} = 875e^{0.0475} = 875 \times 1.048646 = 917.57$$

b)   One futures contract has the value of $250 \times 875 = \$218,750$. Therefore, the number of contracts needed to cover the exposure of $800,000 is: $\$800,000 \div \$218,750 = 3.65714$. Furthermore, we need to adjust for the difference in beta. Since the beta of our portfolio exceeds 1, it moves more than the index in either direction. Therefore, we must increase the number of contracts. The final hedge quantity is: $3.65714 \times 1.1 = 4.02286$. Therefore, we should short-sell 4.02286 S&P 500 index future contracts.

As the correlation between the index and our portfolio is assumed to be one, we have no basis risk and have perfectly hedged our position and transformed it into a riskless investment. Therefore, we expect to earn the risk-free interest rate as a return over one year.

Question 5.18.

The current exchange rate is 0.02E/Y, which implies 50Y/E. The euro continuously compounded interest rate is 0.04, the yen continuously compounded interest rate 0.01. Time to expiration is 0.5 years. Plug the input variables into the formula to see that:

$$\text{Euro/Yen forward} = 0.02e^{(0.04-0.01)\times0.5} = 0.02 \times 1.015113 = 0.020302$$
$$\text{Yen/Euro forward} = 50e^{(0.01-0.04)\times0.5} = 50 \times 0.98511 = 49.2556$$

Question 5.20.

a)   The Eurodollar futures price is 93.23. Therefore, we can use equation (5.20) of the main text to back out the three-month LIBOR rate:

$$r_{91} = (100 - 93.23) \times \frac{1}{100} \times \frac{1}{4} \times \frac{91}{90} = 0.017113.$$

b)   We will have to repay principal plus interest on the loan that we are taking from the following June to September. Because we shorted a Eurodollar futures, we are guaranteed the interest rate we calculated in part a). Therefore, we have a repayment of:

$$\$10,000,000 \times (1 + r_{91}) = \$10,000,000 \times 1.017113 = \$10,171,130$$

Chapter 6
Commodity Forwards and Futures

Question 6.2.

The spot price of oil is $32.00 per barrel. With a continuously compounded annual risk-free rate of 2%, we can again calculate the lease rate according to the formula:

$$\delta_l = r - \frac{1}{T} \ln\left(\frac{F_{0,T}}{S_0}\right)$$

Time to expiration	Forward price	Annualized lease rate
3 months	$31.37	0.0995355
6 months	$30.75	0.0996918
9 months	$30.14	0.0998436
12 months	$29.54	0.0999906

The lease rate is higher than the risk-free interest rate. The forward curve is downward sloping, thus the prices of exercise 6.2. are an example of backwardation.

Question 6.4.

a)   As we need to borrow a pencil to sell it short, we must pay the lender the lease rate for the time we borrow the asset, i.e., until expiration of the contract in one year. After one year, we have to pay back one pencil, which will cost us S_T, the uncertain future pencil price, plus the leasing costs: Total payment $= S_T + S_T \times \left(e^{0.05} - 1\right) = S_T e^{0.05} = 1.05127 \times S_T$.

It does not make sense to store pencils in equilibrium, because even if we have an active lease market for pencils, the lease rate is smaller than the risk-free interest rate. Lending money at ten percent is more profitable than lending pencils at five percent.

b)   The equilibrium forward price is calculated according to our pricing formula:

$$F_{0,T} = S_0 \times e^{(r-\delta_l)\times T} = \$0.20 \times e^{(0.10-0.05)\times 1} = \$0.20 \times 1.05127 = \$0.2103,$$

which is the price given in the exercise.

c)   Let us first look at the different arbitrage strategies we can use in each case.

c1)   Pencils can be sold short. We can engage in our usual reverse cash and carry arbitrage:

Transaction	Time 0	Time T = 1
Long forward	0	$S_T - F_{0,T}$
Short-sell tailed pencil position, @ 0.05	$0.19025	$-S_T$
Lend short-sale proceeds @ 0.1	$-$0.19025	$0.2103
Total	0	$0.2103 - F_{0,T}$

For there to be no arbitrage, $F_{0,T} \geq \$0.2103$

c2)   Suppose pencils cannot be sold short. Then we have no ability to create the short position necessary to offset the pencil price risk from the long forward. Consequently, we are not able to find a lower boundary for the pencil forward in this case.

c3)   Pencils can be loaned. We engage in a cash and carry arbitrage:

Transaction	Time 0	Time T = 1
Short forward	0	$F_{0,T} - S_T$
Buy tailed pencil position, lend @0.05	$-$0.19025	S_T
borrow @ 0.1	$0.19025	$-$0.2103
Total	0	$F_{0,T} - \$0.2103$

For there to be no arbitrage, $F_{0,T} \leq \$0.2103$

c4)   Suppose pencils cannot be loaned. Then our cash and carry arbitrage becomes:

Transaction	Time 0	Time T = 1
Short forward	0	$F_{0,T} - S_T$
Buy pencil	$-$0.20	S_T
borrow @ 0.1	$0.20	$-$0.2210
Total	0	$F_{0,T} - \$0.2210$

For there to be no arbitrage, $F_{0,T} \leq \$0.2210$
Therefore, we have found the following no-arbitrage regions:

	Lower bound on forward	Upper bound on forward
loan=yes, short-sale=yes	$F_{0,T} \geq \$0.2103$	$F_{0,T} \leq \$0.2103$
loan=no, short-sale=yes	$F_{0,T} \geq \$0.2103$	$F_{0,T} \leq \$0.2210$
loan=yes, short-sale=no	—	$F_{0,T} \leq \$0.2103$
loan=no, short-sale=no	—	$F_{0,T} \leq \$0.2210$

Question 6.6.

a) The forward prices reflect a market for widgets in which seasonality is important. Let us look at two examples, one with constant demand and seasonal supply, and another one with constant supply and seasonal demand.

One possible explanation might be that widgets are extremely difficult to produce and that they need one key ingredient that is only available during July/August. However, the demand for the widget is constant throughout the year. In order to be able to sell the widgets throughout the year, widgets must be stored after production in August. The forward curve reflects the ever increasing storage costs of widgets until the next production cycle arrives. Once produced, widget prices fall again to the spot price.

Another story that is consistent with the observed prices of widgets is that widgets are in particularly high demand during the summer months. The storage of widgets may be costly, which means that widget producers are reluctant to build up inventory long before the summer. Storage occurs slowly over the winter months and inventories build up sharply just before the highest demand during the summer months. The forward prices reflect those storage cycle costs.

b) Let us take the December 2001 forward price as a proxy for the spot price in December 2001. We can then calculate with our cash and carry arbitrage tableau:

Transaction	Time 0	Time $T = 3/12$
Short March forward	0	$3.075 - S_T$
Buy December Forward (= Buy spot)	-3.00	S_T
Pay storage cost		-0.03
Total	-3.00	3.045

We can calculate the annualized rate of return as:

$$\frac{3.045}{3.00} = e^{(r) \times T}$$

$$\Leftrightarrow \ln\left(\frac{3.045}{3.00}\right) = r \times 3/12$$

$$r = 0.05955$$

which is the prevailing risk-free interest rate of 0.06. This result seems to make sense.

c) Let us again take the December 2001 forward price as a proxy for the spot price in December 2001. We can then calculate with our cash and carry arbitrage tableau:

Transaction	Time 0	Time T= 9/12
Short Sep forward	0	$2.75 - S_T$
Buy spot	-3.00	S_T
Pay storage cost Sep		-0.03
FV(Storage Jun)		-0.0305
FV(Storage Mar)		-0.0309
Total	-3.00	2.6586

We can calculate the annualized rate of return as:

$$\frac{2.6586}{3.00} = e^{(r) \times T} \Leftrightarrow \ln\left(\frac{2.6586}{3.00}\right) = r \times 9/12$$

$$r = -0.16108$$

This result does not seem to make sense. We would earn a negative annualized return of 16% on such a cash and carry arbitrage. Therefore, it is likely that our naive calculations do not capture an important fact about the widget market. In particular, we will buy and hold the widget through a time where the forward curve indicates that there is a significant convenience yield attached to widgets.

It is tempting, although premature, to conclude that a reverse cash and carry arbitrage may make a positive 16 % annualized return. Question 6.7. deals with this aspect.

Question 6.8.

a) The first possibility is a simple cash and carry arbitrage:

Transaction	Time 0	Time T = 3/12
Short March forward	0	$3.10 - S_T$
Buy December forward (= Buy spot)	-3.00	S_T
Borrow @ 6%	$+3.00$	-3.045
Pay storage cost		-0.03
Total	0	$+0.025$

The second possibility involves using the June futures contract. It is a forward cash and carry strategy:

Transaction	Time = T(1) = 3/12	Time = T(2) = 6/12
Short March forward	$3.10 - S_{T(1)}$	$-S_{T(2)}$
Buy June forward	0	$S_{T(2)} - 3.152$
Lend @ 6%	-3.10	3.1469
Receive storage cost		$+0.03$
Total	0	$+0.02485$

We can use the June futures in our calculations and claim to receive storage costs, because it is easy to show that the value of it is reflecting the negative lease rate of the storage costs.

b)   It is not possible to undertake an arbitrage with the futures contracts that expire prior to September 2002. A decrease in the September futures value means that we would need to buy the September futures contract, and any arbitrage strategy would need some short position in the widget. However, the drop in the futures price in September indicates that there is a significant convenience yield factored into the futures price over the period June–September. As we have no information about it, it is not possible for us to guarantee that we find a lender of widgets at a favorable lease rate to follow through our arbitrage trading program. The decrease in the September futures may in fact reflect an increase in the opportunity costs of widget owners.

Question 6.10.

Our best bet for the current spot price is the first available forward price, properly discounted by taking the interest rate and the lease rate into account, and by ignoring any storage cost and convenience yield (because we do not have any information on it):

$$F_{0,T} = S_0 \times e^{(r-\delta_l) \times T}$$
$$\Leftrightarrow \quad S_0 = F_{0,T} \times e^{-(r-\delta_l) \times T}$$
$$\Leftrightarrow \quad S_0 = 313.81 \times e^{-(0.06-0.015) \times 1} = 313.81 \times 0.956 = 300.0016$$

Chapter 7
Interest Rate Forwards and Futures

Question 7.2.

The coupon bond pays a coupon of $60 each year plus the principal of $1,000 after five years. We have cash flows of [60, 60, 60, 60, 1060]. To obtain the price of the coupon bond, we multiply each cash flow by the zero-coupon bond price of that year. This yields a bond price of $1,037.25280.

Question 7.4.

Maturity	Zero-Coupon Bond Yield	Zero Coupon Bond Price	One-Year Implied Forward Rate	Par Coupon	Cont. Comp. Zero Yield
1	0.05000	0.95238	0.05000	0.05000	0.04879
2	0.04200	0.92101	0.03406	0.04216	0.04114
3	0.04000	0.88900	0.03601	0.04018	0.03922
4	0.03600	0.86808	0.02409	0.03634	0.03537
5	0.02900	0.86681	0.00147	0.02962	0.02859

Question 7.6.

In order to be able to solve this problem, it is best to take equation (7.6) of the main text and solve progressively for all zero-coupon bond prices, starting with year one. This yields the series of zero-coupon bond prices from which we can proceed as usual to determine the yields.

Maturity	Zero-Coupon Bond Yield	Zero Coupon Bond Price	One-Year Implied Forward Rate	Par Coupon	Cont. Comp. Zero Yield
1	0.03000	0.97087	0.03000	0.03000	0.02956
2	0.03500	0.93352	0.04002	0.03491	0.03440
3	0.04000	0.88899	0.05009	0.03974	0.03922
4	0.04700	0.83217	0.06828	0.04629	0.04593
5	0.05300	0.77245	0.07732	0.05174	0.05164

Question 7.8.

a)   We have to take into account the interest we (or our counterparty) can earn on the FRA settlement if we settle the loan on initiation day, and not on the actual repayment day. Therefore,

46

we tail the FRA settlement by the prevailing market interest rate of 5%. The dollar settlement is:

$$\frac{\left(r_{annually} - r_{FRA}\right)}{1 + r_{annually}} \times \text{notional principal} = \frac{(0.05 - 0.06)}{1 + 0.05} \times \$500{,}000.00 = -\$4{,}761.905$$

b)   If the FRA is settled on the date the loan is repaid (or settled in arrears), the settlement amount is determined by:

$$\left(r_{annually} - r_{FRA}\right) \times \text{notional principal} = (0.05 - 0.06) \times \$500{,}000.00 = -\$5{,}000$$

We have to pay at the settlement, because the interest rate we could borrow at is 5%, but we have agreed via the FRA to a borrowing rate of 6%. Interest rates moved in an unfavorable direction.

Question 7.10.

We can find the implied forward rates using the following formula:

$$\left[1 + r_0\left(t, t + s\right)\right] = \frac{P\left(0, t\right)}{P\left(0, t + s\right)}$$

This yields the following rates on the synthetic FRAs:

$$r_0\left(90, 180\right) = \frac{0.99009}{0.97943} - 1 = 0.010884$$

$$r_0\left(90, 270\right) = \frac{0.99009}{0.96525} - 1 = 0.025734$$

$$r_0\left(90, 360\right) = \frac{0.99009}{0.95238} - 1 = 0.039596$$

Question 7.12.

We can find the implied forward rate using the following formula:

$$\left[1 + r_0\left(t, t + s\right)\right] = \frac{P\left(0, t\right)}{P\left(0, t + s\right)}$$

With the numbers of the exercise, this yields:

$$r_0\left(270, 360\right) = \frac{0.96525}{0.95238} - 1 = 0.0135135$$

The following table follows the textbook in looking at forward agreements from a borrower's perspective, i.e. a borrower goes long on an FRA to hedge his position, and a lender is thus short the FRA. Since we are the counterparty for a lender, we are in fact the borrower, and thus long the forward rate agreement.

Transaction today	$t = 0$	$t = 270$	$t = 360$
Enter long FRAU		10M	$-10M \times 1.013514$ $= -10.13514M$
Sell 9.6525M Zero Coupons maturing at time $t = 180$	9.6525M	$-10M$	
Buy $(1 + 0.013514) * 10M * 0.95238$ Zero Coupons maturing at time $t = 360$	$-10M \times 1.013514$ $\times 0.95238 = -9.6525M$		$+10.13514M$
TOTAL	0	0	0

By entering in the above mentioned positions, we are perfectly hedged against the risk of the FRA. Please note that we are making use of the fact that interest rates are perfectly predictable.

Question 7.14.

We would like to guarantee the return of 6.5%. We receive payments 6.95485 after year one and year two, and a payment of 106.95485 after year three. If interest rates are uncertain, we face an interest rate risk for the investment of the first coupon from year one to year two and for the discounting of the final payment from year three to year one.

Suppose we enter into a forward rate agreement to lend 6.95484 from year one to year two at the current forward rate from year one to year two, and we enter into a forward rate agreement to borrow 106.95485 tailed by the prevailing forward rate for year two to year three, at the prevailing forward rate. This leads to the following cash-flow table:

Transaction today	$t = 0$	$t = 1$	$t = 2$	$t = 3$
Buy 3-year par bond	-100			
Receive first coupon	0	6.95485		
Enter short FRAU	0	-6.95485	6.95485×1.0700237	
Receive second coupon	0		6.95485	
Enter long FRA for tailed position	0		$106.95485/1.0800705$ $= 99.025804$	-106.95485
Receive final coupon and principal	0			106.95485
TOTAL	-100	0	113.4225	0

We see that we can secure the same gross return as in the previous question, $\sqrt{113.4225 \div 100} = 1.065$. By entering appropriate FRAs, we secured the desired return of 6.5%. Please note that we made use of the fact that we knew that we wanted to undo the position at $t = 2$.

Question 7.16.

a)   The implied LIBOR of the September Eurodollar futures of 96.4 is: $\dfrac{100 - 96.4}{400} = 0.9\%$

b)   As we want to borrow money, we want to buy protection against high interest rates, which means low Eurodollar future prices. We will short the Eurodollar contract.

c)   One Eurodollar contract is based on a $1 million 3-month deposit. As we want to hedge a loan of $50M, we will enter into 50 short contracts.

d)   A true 3-month LIBOR of 1% means an annualized position (annualized by market conventions) of $1\% * 4 = 4\%$. Therefore, our 50 short contracts will pay:

$$\left[96.4 - (100 - 4) \times 100 \times \$25\right] \times 50 = \$50,000$$

The increase in the interest rate has made our loan more expensive. The futures position that we entered to hedge the interest rate exposure, compensates for this increase. In particular, we pay $\$50,000,000 \times 0.01 - payoff\ futures = \$500,000 - \$50,000 = \$450,000$, which corresponds to the 0.9% we sought to lock in.

Question 7.18.

a)   We face the classic problem of asset mismatch. We are interested in locking in an interest rate for a 150-day investment, 60 days from now. However, while the Eurodollar futures matures 60 days from now, it secures a lending rate for 90 days. We face the problem that the 90-day and 150-day interest rates may not be perfectly correlated. (For example, the term structure could, over the next 60 days, move from upward sloping to downward sloping).

b)   As we want to lend money, we want to buy protection against low interest rates, which means high Eurodollar future prices. We will therefore long the Eurodollar contract.

c)   The implied LIBOR of the September Eurodollar futures of 94 is: $\dfrac{100 - 94}{400} = 1.5\%$. Under the assumption that the 3-month LIBOR rate and the 150-day interest rate are based on the same annualized interest rate of 6%, we are able to lock in an interest rate of: $1.5\% \times \dfrac{150}{90} = 2.5\%$. Please note that this is a rather strong assumption.

d)   One Eurodollar futures contract is based on a $1 million 3-month deposit. As we want to hedge an investment of $100M, we will enter into 100 long contracts. Again, we are making the strong assumption that the annualized 3-month LIBOR rate and the annualized 150 day rate are identical and perfectly correlated.

Question 7.20.

We will use the Excel functions Duration and Mduration to calculate the required durations. They are of the form:

MDURATION(Start Date; Terminal Date; Coupon; Yield; Frequency)
DURATION(Start Date; Terminal Date; Coupon; Yield; Frequency),

where frequency determines the number of coupon payments per year. In order to use the function, we have to give Excel a start date and terminal date, but we can just pick two dates that are exactly the requested number of years apart. Plugging in the values of the exercises yields:

a)   Macaulay Duration $= 4.59324084$
       Modified Duration $= 4.3983078$

b)   Macaulay Duration $= 5.99377496$
       Modified Duration $= 5.73566981$

c)   We need to find the yield to maturity of this bond first. We can do so by using the YIELD function of Excel. Plugging in the relevant values, we get: Yield $= 0.07146759$. Now we can again use the Mduration and Duration formulas. This yields:

       Macaulay Duration $= 7.6955970$
       Modified Duration $= 7.1822957$

Question 7.22.

We will exploit equation (7.13) of the main text to find the optimal hedge ratio:

$$N = -\frac{D_1 B_1(y_1)/(1+y_1)}{D_2 B_2(y_2)/(1+y_2)} = \frac{6.631864 \times 106.44/(1.05004)}{7.098302 \times 112.29/(1.05252)} = -\frac{672.255918}{757.2951883} = -0.887707$$

Therefore, we have to short 0.887707 units of the nine-year bond for every eight-year bond to obtain a duration-matched portfolio.

Question 7.24.

a)   Compute the convexity of a 3-year bond paying annual coupons of 4.5% and selling at par.

For a par bond, the yield to maturity is equal to the coupon, or 4.5% in our case. We can calculate the convexity based on the formula:

$$
\begin{aligned}
\text{Convexity} &= \frac{1}{B(y)}\left[\sum_{i=1}^{n} \frac{i(i+1)}{m^2} \frac{C/m}{(1+y/m)^{i+2}} + \frac{n(n+1)}{m^2} \frac{M}{(1+y/m)^{n+2}}\right] \\
&= \frac{1}{100}\left[\frac{1(1+1)}{1^2} \frac{4.5/1}{(1+0.045)^{1+2}} + \frac{2(2+1)}{1^2} \frac{4.5/1}{(1+0.045)^{2+2}} \right. \\
&\quad \left. + \frac{3(3+1)}{1^2} \frac{104.5}{(1+0.045/1)^{3+2}}\right] \\
&= 10.3680
\end{aligned}
$$

b)   Compute the convexity of a 3-year 4.5% coupon bond that makes semiannual coupon payments and that currently sells at par.

Now, $m = 2$. We have $n = m * T = 2 * 3 = 6$. The convexity is:

$$
\begin{aligned}
\text{Convexity} &= \frac{1}{B(y)} \left[\sum_{i=1}^{n} \frac{i\,(i+1)}{m^2} \frac{C/m}{(1+y/m)^{i+2}} + \frac{n\,(n+1)}{m^2} \frac{M}{(1+y/m)^{n+2}} \right] \\
&= \frac{1}{100} \left[\frac{1\,(1+1)}{2^2} \frac{2.25/1}{(1+0.0225)^{1+2}} + \frac{2\,(2+1)}{2^2} \frac{2.25/1}{(1+0.0225)^{2+2}} \right. \\
&\quad + \frac{3\,(3+1)}{2^2} \frac{2.25/1}{(1+0.0225)^{3+2}} + \frac{4\,(4+1)}{2^2} \frac{2.25/1}{(1+0.0225)^{4+2}} \\
&\quad \left. + \frac{5\,(5+1)}{2^2} \frac{2.25/1}{(1+0.0225)^{5+2}} + \frac{6\,(6+1)}{2^2} \frac{102.25}{(1+0.0225/1)^{6+2}} \right] \\
&= 9.3302
\end{aligned}
$$

c)   Is the convexity different in the two cases? Why?

Yes, the convexity for the semi-annual bond is smaller. We spread the bond payments out over more periods, which makes the bond's duration slightly less susceptible to interest rate changes.

Chapter 8
Swaps

Question 8.2.

a)   We first solve for the present value of the cost per three barrels, based on the forward prices:

$$\frac{\$20}{1.06} + \frac{\$21}{(1.065)^2} + \frac{\$22}{(1.07)^3} = 55.3413.$$

We then obtain the swap price per barrel by solving:

$$\frac{x}{1.06} + \frac{x}{(1.065)^2} + \frac{x}{(1.07)^3} = 55.341$$

$$\Leftrightarrow \qquad\qquad\qquad\qquad x = 20.9519$$

b)   We first solve for the present value of the cost per two barrels (year 2 and year 3):

$$\frac{\$21}{(1.065)^2} + \frac{\$22}{(1.07)^3} = 36.473.$$

We then obtain the swap price per barrel by solving:

$$\frac{x}{(1.065)^2} + \frac{x}{(1.07)^3} = 36.473$$

$$\Leftrightarrow \quad x \qquad\qquad\qquad = 21.481$$

Question 8.4.

The fair swap rate was determined to be $20.952. Therefore, compared to the forward curve price of $20 in one year, we are overpaying $0.952. In year two, this overpayment has increased to $0.952 \times 1.070024 = 1.01866$, where we used the appropriate forward rate to calculate the interest payment. In year two, we underpay by $0.048, so that our total accumulative underpayment is $0.97066. In year three, this overpayment has increased again to $0.97066 \times 1.08007 = 1.048$. However, in year three, we receive a fixed payment of 20.952, which underpays relative to the forward curve price of $22 by $22 - \$20.952 = 1.048$. Therefore, our cumulative balance is indeed zero, which was to be shown.

Question 8.6.

In order to answer this question, we use equation (8.13.) of the main text. We assumed that the interest rates and the corresponding zero-coupon bonds were:

Quarter	Interest rate	Zero-coupon price
1	0.0150	0.9852
2	0.0302	0.9707
3	0.0457	0.9563
4	0.0614	0.9422
5	0.0773	0.9283
6	0.0934	0.9145
7	0.1098	0.9010
8	0.1265	0.8877

Using formula 8.13., we obtain the following per barrel swap prices:

4-quarter swap price: $20.8533

8-quarter swap price: $20.4284

The total costs of prepaid 4- and 8-quarter swaps are the present values of the payment obligations. They are:

4-quarter prepaid swap price: $80.3768

8-quarter prepaid swap price: $152.9256

Question 8.8.

We use formula (8.4), and replace the forward interest rate with the forward oil prices. In particular, we calculate:

$$X = \frac{\sum_{i=3}^{6} P_0(0, t_i) F_{0,t_i}}{\sum_{i=3}^{6} P_0(0, t_i)} = \$20.3807$$

Therefore, the swap price of a 4-quarter oil swap with the first settlement occurring in the third quarter is $20.3807.

Question 8.10.

We use equation (8.6) of the main text to answer this question:

$$X = \frac{\sum_{i=1}^{8} Q_{t_i} P_0(0, t_i) F_{0,t_i}}{\sum_{i=1}^{8} Q_{t_i} P_0(0, t_i)}, \text{ where } Q = [1, 2, 1, 2, 1, 2, 1, 2]$$

After plugging in the relevant variables given in the exercise, we obtain a value of $20.4099 for the swap price.

Question 8.12.

With a swap price of $2.2044, and the forward prices of question 8.11., we can calculate the implied loan amount. We can calculate the net position by subtracting the swap price from the forward prices. The 1-quarter implied forward rate is calculated from the zero-coupon bond prices. The column implicit loan balance adds the net position each quarter and the implicit loan balance plus interest of the previous quarter. Please note that the shape of the forward curve—we are initially loaning money, because the swap price is lower than the forward price.

Quarter	Forward price	Net balance	Forward interest rate	Implicit loan balance
1	2.25	0.0456	1.0150	0.0456
2	2.60	0.3955	1.0156	0.4418
3	2.20	−0.0042	1.0162	0.4447
4	1.90	−0.3046	1.0168	0.1476
5	2.20	−0.0043	1.0170	0.1458
6	2.50	0.2954	1.0172	0.4437
7	2.15	−0.0543	1.0175	0.3971
8	1.80	−0.4042	1.0178	0.0000

Question 8.14.

From the given zero-coupon bond prices, we can calculate the one-quarter forward interest rates. They are:

Quarter	Forward interest rate
1	1.0150
2	1.0156
3	1.0162
4	1.0168
5	1.0170
6	1.0172
7	1.0175
8	1.0178

Now, we can calculate the swap prices for 4 and 8 quarters according to the formula:

$$X = \frac{\sum_{i=1}^{n} P_0\,(0, t_i) r_0\,(t_{i-1}, t_i)}{\sum_{i=1}^{n} P_0\,(0, t_i)}, \quad \text{where } n = 4 \text{ or } 8$$

This yields the following prices:

4-quarter fixed swap price: 1.59015%

8-quarter fixed swap price: 1.66096%

Question 8.16.

The dollar zero-coupon bond prices for the three years are:

$$P_{0,1} = \frac{1}{1.06} = 0.9434$$

$$P_{0,2} = \frac{1}{(1.06)^2} = 0.8900$$

$$P_{0,3} = \frac{1}{(1.06)^3} = 0.8396$$

R^* is 0.035, the Euro-bond coupon rate. The current exchange rate is 0.9\$/E. Plugging all the above variables into formula (8.9) indeed yields 0.06, the dollar coupon rate:

$$R = \frac{\sum_{i=1}^{3} P_0\,(0,t_i)\,R^* F_{0,t_i}/x_0 + P_{0,3}\left(F_{0,t_n}/x_0 - 1\right)}{\sum_{i=1}^{3} P_0\,(0,t_i)} = \frac{0.098055 + 0.062317}{2.673} = 0.060$$

Question 8.18.

We can use equation (8.9), but there is a complication: We do not have the current spot exchange rate. However, it is possible to back it out by using the methodology of the previous chapters: We know that the following relation must hold:

$$F_{0,1} = X_0 e^{(r-r^*)}, \text{ where the interest rates are already on a quarterly level.}$$

We can back out the interest rates from the given zero-coupon prices. Doing so yields a current exchange rate of 0.90 \$/Euro. $R*$ is the 8-quarter fixed swap price payment of 0.0094572.

By plugging in all the relevant variables into equation 8.9, we can indeed see that this yields a swap rate of 1.66%, which is the same rate that we calculated in exercise 8.14.

Chapter 9
Parity and Other Option Relationships

Question 9.2.

This problem requires the application of put-call-parity. We have:

$$S_0 - C(30, 0.5) + P(30, 0.5) - e^{-rT}30 = PV(dividends)$$
$$\Leftrightarrow \quad PV(dividends) = 32 - 4.29 + 2.64 - 29.406 = \$0.944.$$

Question 9.4.

We can make use of the put-call-parity for currency options:

$$+P(K, T) = -e^{-r_f T}x_0 + C(K, T) + e^{-rT}K$$
$$\Leftrightarrow \quad P(K, T) = -e^{-0.04}0.95 + 0.0571 + e^{-0.06}.93 = -0.91275 + 0.0571 + 0.87584 = 0.0202.$$

A \$0.93 strike European put option has a value of \$0.0202.

Question 9.6.

a)   We can use put-call-parity to determine the forward price:

$$+C(K, T) - P(K, T) = PV(forward\ price) - PV(strike) = e^{-rT}F_{0,T} - Ke^{-rT}$$
$$\Leftrightarrow \quad F_{0,T} = e^{rT}\left[+C(K, T) - P(K, T) + Ke^{-rT}\right]$$
$$= e^{0.05*0.5}\left[\$0.0404 - \$0.0141 + \$0.9e^{-0.05*0.5}\right]$$
$$\Leftrightarrow \quad F_{0,T} = \$0.92697.$$

b)   Given the forward price from above and the pricing formula for the forward price, we can find the current spot rate:

$$F_{0,T} = x_0 e^{(r-r_f)T}$$
$$\Leftrightarrow \quad x_0 = F_{0,T}e^{-(r-r_f)T} = \$0.92697e^{-(0.05-0.035)0.5} = \$0.92.$$

Question 9.8.

Both equations (9.13) and (9.14) are violated. We use a call bull spread and a put bear spread to profit from these arbitrage opportunities.

Transaction	$t = 0$	$S_T < 50$	$50 \leq S_T \leq 55$	$S_T > 55$
			Expiration or Exercise	
Buy 50 strike call	-9	0	$S_T - 50$	$S_T - 50$
Sell 55 strike call	$+10$	0	0	$55 - S_T$
TOTAL	$+1$	0	$S_T - 50 > 0$	$5 > 0$

Transaction	$t = 0$	$S_T < 50$	$50 \leq S_T \leq 55$	$S_T > 55$
			Expiration or Exercise	
Buy 55 strike put	-6	$55 - S_T$	$55 - S_T$	0
Sell 50 strike put	7	$S_T - 50$	0	0
TOTAL	$+1$	$5 > 0$	$55 - S_T > 0$	0

Please note that we initially receive money, and that at expiration the profit is non-negative. We have found arbitrage opportunities.

Question 9.10.

Both equations (9.17) and (9.18) of the textbook are violated. To see this, let us calculate the values. We have:

$$\frac{C(K_1) - C(K_2)}{K_2 - K_1} = \frac{18 - 14}{55 - 50} = 0.8 \quad \text{and} \quad \frac{C(K_2) - C(K_3)}{K_3 - K_2} = \frac{14 - 9.50}{60 - 55} = 0.9,$$

which violates equation (9.17) and

$$\frac{P(K_2) - P(K_1)}{K_2 - K_1} = \frac{10.75 - 7}{55 - 50} = 0.75 \quad \text{and} \quad \frac{P(K_3) - P(K_2)}{K_3 - K_2} = \frac{14.45 - 10.75}{60 - 55} = 0.74,$$

which violates equation (9.18).

We calculate lambda in order to know how many options to buy and sell when we construct the butterfly spread that exploits this form of mispricing. Because the strike prices are symmetric around 55, lambda is equal to 0.5.

Therefore, we use a call and put butterfly spread to profit from these arbitrage opportunities.

Transaction	$t = 0$	$S_T < 50$	$50 \leq S_T \leq 55$	$55 \leq S_T \leq 60$	$S_T > 60$
Buy 1 50 strike call	-18	0	$S_T - 50$	$S_T - 50$	$S_T - 50$
Sell 2 55 strike calls	$+28$	0	0	$110 - 2 \times S_T$	$110 - 2 \times S_T$
Buy 1 60 strike call	-9.50	0	0	0	$S_T - 60$
TOTAL	$+0.50$	0	$S_T - 50 \geq 0$	$60 - S_T \geq 0$	0

Transaction	$t = 0$	$S_T < 50$	$50 \leq S_T \leq 55$	$55 \leq S_T \leq 60$	$S_T > 60$
Buy 1 50 strike put	-7	$50 - S_T$	0	0	0
Sell 2 55 strike puts	21.50	$2 \times S_T - 110$	$2 \times S_T - 110$	0	0
Buy 1 60 strike put	-14.45	$60 - S_T$	$60 - S_T$	$60 - S_T$	0
TOTAL	$+0.05$	0	$S_T - 50 \geq 0$	$60 - S_T \geq 0$	0

Please note that we initially receive money and have non-negative future payoffs. Therefore, we have found an arbitrage possibility, independent of the prevailing interest rate.

Question 9.12.

a)   Equation (9.15) of the textbook is violated. We use a call bear spread to profit from this arbitrage opportunity.

			Expiration or Exercise	
Transaction	$t = 0$	$S_T < 90$	$90 \leq S_T \leq 95$	$S_T > 95$
Sell 90 strike call	$+10$	0	$90 - S_T$	$90 - S_T$
Buy 95 strike call	-4	0	0	$S_T - 95$
TOTAL	$+6$	0	$90 - S_T > -5$	-5

Please note that we initially receive more money than our biggest possible exposure in the future. Therefore, we have found an arbitrage possibility, independent of the prevailing interest rate.

b)   Now, equation (9.15) is not violated anymore. However, we can still construct an arbitrage opportunity, given the information in the exercise. We continue to sell the 90-strike call and buy the 95-strike call, and we loan our initial positive net balance for two years until expiration. It is important that the options be European, because otherwise we would not be able to tell whether the 90-strike call could be exercised against us sometime (note that we do not have information regarding any dividends).

We have the following arbitrage table:

			Expiration $t = T$	
Transaction	$t = 0$	$S_T < 90$	$90 \leq S_T \leq 95$	$S_T > 95$
Sell 90 strike call	$+10$	0	$90 - S_T$	$90 - S_T$
Buy 95 strike call	-5.25	0	0	$S_T - 95$
Loan 4.75	-4.75	5.80	5.80	5.8
TOTAL	0	5.80	$95.8 - S_T > 0$	$+0.8$

In all possible future states, we have a strictly positive payoff. We have created something out of nothing—we demonstrated arbitrage.

c)   We will first verify that equation (9.17) is violated. We have:

$$\frac{C(K_1) - C(K_2)}{K_2 - K_1} = \frac{15 - 10}{100 - 90} = 0.5 \quad \text{and} \quad \frac{C(K_2) - C(K_3)}{K_3 - K_2} = \frac{10 - 6}{105 - 100} = 0.8,$$

which violates equation (9.17).

We calculate lambda in order to know how many options to buy and sell when we construct the butterfly spread that exploits this form of mispricing. Using formula (9.19), we can calculate that lambda is equal to 1/3. To buy and sell round lots, we multiply all the option trades by 3.

We use an asymmetric call and put butterfly spread to profit from these arbitrage opportunities.

Transaction	$t = 0$	$S_T < 90$	$90 \leq S_T \leq 100$	$100 \leq S_T \leq 105$	$S_T > 105$
Buy 1 90 strike calls	-15	0	$S_T - 90$	$S_T - 90$	$S_T - 90$
Sell 3 100 strike calls	$+30$	0	0	$300 - 3 \times S_T$	$300 - 3 \times S_T$
Buy 2 105 strike calls	-12	0	0	0	$2 \times S_T - 210$
TOTAL	$+3$	0	$S_T - 90 \geq 0$	$210 - 2 \times S_T \geq 0$	0

We indeed have an arbitrage opportunity.

Question 9.14.

This question is closely related to question 9.13. In this exercise, the strike is not cash anymore, but rather one share of Apple. In parts a) and b), there is no benefit in keeping Apple longer, because the dividend is zero.

a)   The underlying asset is the stock of Apple, which does not pay a dividend. Therefore, we have an American call option on a non-dividend-paying stock. It is never optimal to early exercise such an option.

b)   The underlying asset is the stock of Apple, and the strike consists of AOL. As AOL does not pay a dividend, the interest rate on AOL is zero. We will therefore never early exercise the put option, because we cannot receive earlier any benefits associated with holding Apple – there are none. If Apple is bankrupt, there is no loss from not early exercising, because the option is worth max[0, AOL – 0], which is equivalent to one share of AOL, because of the limited liability of stock. As AOL does not pay dividends, we are indifferent between holding the option and the stock.

c)   For the American call option, dividends on the stock are the reason why we want to receive the stock earlier, and now Apple pays a dividend. We usually benefit from waiting, because we can continue to earn interest on the strike. However, in this case, the dividend on AOL remains zero, so we do not have this benefit associated with waiting to exercise. Finally, we saw that there is a second benefit to waiting: the insurance protection, which will not be affected by the zero AOL dividend. Therefore, there now may be circumstances in which we will early exercise, but we will not always early exercise.

For the American put option, there is no cost associated with waiting to exercise the option, because exercising gives us a share of AOL, which does not pay interest in form of a dividend. However, by early exercising we will forego the interest we could earn on Apple. Therefore, it is again never optimal to exercise the American put option early.

Question 9.16.

Short call perspective:

Transaction	$t = 0$	time $= T$ $S_T \leq K$	time $= T$ $S_T > K$
Sell call	$+C^B$	0	$K - S_T$
Buy put	$-P^A$	$K - S_T$	0
Buy share	$-S^A$	S_T	S_T
Borrow @ r_B	$+Ke^{-r_B T}$	$-K$	$-K$
TOTAL	$C^B - P^A - S^A + Ke^{-r_B T}$	0	0

In order to preclude arbitrage, we must have: $C^B - P^A - S^A + Ke^{-r_B T} \leq 0$.

Long call perspective:

Transaction	$t = 0$	time $= T$ $S_T \leq K$	time $= T$ $S_T > K$
Buy call	$-C^A$	0	$S_T - K$
Sell put	$+P^B$	$S_T - K$	0
Sell share	$+S^B$	$-S_T$	$-S_T$
Lend @ r_L	$-Ke^{-r_L T}$	$+K$	$+K$
TOTAL	$-C^A + P^B + S^B - Ke^{-r_L T}$	0	0

In order to preclude arbitrage, we must have: $-C^A + P^B + S^B - Ke^{-r_L T} \leq 0$.

Question 9.18.

Consider the January 80, 85, and 90 call option prices in Table 9.1.

a)   Does convexity hold if you buy a butterfly spread, buying at the ask price and selling at the bid?

Since the strike prices are symmetric, lambda is equal to 0.5. Therefore, to buy a long butterfly spread, we buy the 80-strike call, sell two 85 strike calls and buy one 90 strike call.

$$\frac{C(K_1) - C(K_2)}{K_2 - K_1} = \frac{6.70 - 3.20}{85 - 80} = 0.7 \quad \text{and} \quad \frac{C(K_2) - C(K_3)}{K_3 - K_2} = \frac{3.20 - 1.35}{90 - 85} = 0.37$$

Convexity holds.

b)

$$\frac{C(K_1) - C(K_2)}{K_2 - K_1} = \frac{6.5 - 3.4}{85 - 80} = 0.62 \quad \text{and} \quad \frac{C(K_2) - C(K_3)}{K_3 - K_2} = \frac{3.4 - 1.20}{90 - 85} = 0.44$$

Convexity holds.

c)	Does convexity hold if you are a market-maker either buying or selling a butterfly, paying the bid and receiving the ask?

A market maker can buy a butterfly spread at the prices we sell it for. Therefore, the above convexity conditions are the ones relevant for market makers. Convexity is not violated from a market maker's perspective.

Chapter 10
Binomial Option Pricing: I

Question 10.2.

a)   Using the formulas of the textbook, we obtain the following results:

$$\Delta = 0.7$$
$$B = -53.8042$$
$$price = 16.1958$$

b)   If we observe a price of $17, then the option price is too high relative to its theoretical value. We sell the option and synthetically create a call option for $19.196. In order to do so, we buy 0.7 units of the share and borrow $53.804. These transactions yield no risk and a profit of $0.804.

c)   If we observe a price of $15.50, then the option price is too low relative to its theoretical value. We buy the option and synthetically create a short position in an option. In order to do so, we sell 0.7 units of the share and lend $53.8042. These transactions yield no risk and a profit of $0.696.

Question 10.4.

The stock prices evolve according to the following picture:

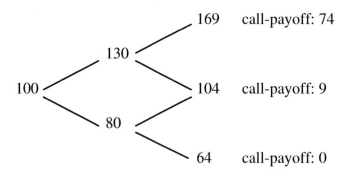

Since we have two binomial steps, and a time to expiration of one year, h is equal to 0.5. Therefore, we can calculate with the usual formulas for the respective nodes:

$t = 0, S = 100$	$t = 1, S = 80$	$t = 1, S = 130$
$\Delta = 0.691$	$\Delta = 0.225$	$\Delta = 1$
$B = -49.127$	$B = -13.835$	$B = -91.275$
$price = 19.994$	$price = 4.165$	$price = 38.725$

Question 10.6.

The stock prices evolve according to the following picture:

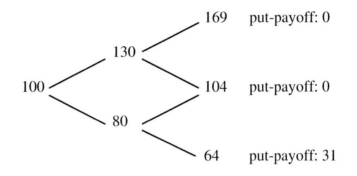

169   put-payoff: 0

130

100   104   put-payoff: 0

80

64   put-payoff: 31

Since we have two binomial steps, and a time to expiration of one year, h is equal to 0.5. Therefore, we can calculate with the usual formulas for the respective nodes:

$t = 0, S = 100$	$t = 1, S = 80$	$t = 1, S = 130$
$\Delta = -0.3088$	$\Delta = -0.775$	$\Delta = 0$
$B = 38.569$	$B = 77.4396$	$B = 0$
$price = 7.6897$	$price = 15.4396$	$price = 0$

Question 10.8.

We must compare the results of the equivalent European put that we calculated in exercise 10.6. with the value of immediate exercise. In 10.6., we calculated:

$t = 1, S = 80$	$t = 1, S = 130$
$\Delta = -0.775$	$\Delta = 0$
$B = 77.4396$	$B = 0$
$price = 15.4396$	$price = 0$
immediate exercise $=$	immediate exercise
$\max(95 - 80, 0) = 15$	$= \max(95 - 130, 0) = 0$

Since the value of immediate exercise is smaller than or equal to the continuation value (of the European options) at both nodes of the tree, there is no benefit to exercising the options before expiration. Therefore, we use the European option values when calculating the $t = 0$ option price:

$$t = 0, S = 100$$

$$\Delta = -0.3088$$

$$B = 38.569$$

$$price = 7.6897$$

$$\text{immediate exercise} = \max(95 - 100, 0) = 0$$

Since the option price is again higher than the value of immediate exercise (which is zero), there is no benefit to exercising the option at $t = 0$. Since it is never optimal to exercise earlier, the early exercise option has no value. The value of the American put option is identical to the value of the European put option.

Question 10.10.

a)   We can calculate for the different nodes of the tree:

	node uu	node ud = du	node dd
delta	1	0.8966	0
B	−92.5001	−79.532	0
call premium	56.6441	15.0403	0
value of early exercise	54.1442	10.478	0

Using these values at the previous node and at the initial node yields:

	$t = 0$	node d	node u
delta	0.7400	0.4870	0.9528
B	−55.7190	−35.3748	−83.2073
call premium	18.2826	6.6897	33.1493
value of early exercise	5	0	27.1250

Please note that in all instances the value of immediate exercise is smaller than the continuation value, the (European) call premium. Therefore, the value of the European call and the American call are identical.

b)   We can calculate similarly the binomial prices at each node in the tree. We can calculate for the different nodes of the tree:

	node uu	node $ud = du$	node dd
delta	0	−0.1034	−1
B	0	12.968	92.5001
put premium	0	2.0624	17.904
value of early exercise	0	0	20.404

Using these values at the previous node and at the initial node yields:

	$t = 0$	node d	node u
delta	-0.26	-0.513	-0.047
B	31.977	54.691	6.859
put premium	5.979	10.387	1.091
value of early exercise	0	8.6307	0

c)   From the previous tables, we can see that at the node dd, it is optimal to early exercise the American put option, because the value of early exercise exceeds the continuation value. Therefore, we must use the value of 20.404 in all relevant previous nodes when we back out the prices of the American put option. We have for nodes d and 0 (the other nodes remain unchanged):

	$t = 0$	node d
delta	-0.297	-0.594
B	36.374	63.005
put premium	6.678	11.709
value of early exercise	0	8.6307

The price of the American put option is indeed 6.678.

Question 10.12.

a)   We can calculate u and d as follows:

$$u = e^{(r-\delta)h+\sigma\sqrt{h}} = e^{(0.08)\times0.25+0.3\times\sqrt{0.25}} = 1.1853$$

$$d = e^{(r-\delta)h-\sigma\sqrt{h}} = e^{(0.08)\times0.25-0.3\times\sqrt{0.25}} = 0.8781$$

b)   We need to calculate the values at the relevant nodes in order to price the European call option:

	$t = 0$	node d	node u
delta	0.6074	0.1513	1
B	-20.187	-4.5736	-39.208
call premium	4.110	0.7402	8.204

c)   We can calculate at the relevant nodes (or, equivalently, you can use put-call-parity for the European put option):

European put	$t = 0$	node d	node u
delta	-0.3926	-0.8487	0
B	18.245	34.634	0
put premium	2.5414	4.8243	0

For the American put option, we have to compare the premia at each node with the value of early exercise. We see from the following table that at the node d, it is advantageous to exercise the option early; consequently, we use the value of early exercise when we calculate the value of the put option.

American put	$t = 0$	node d	node u
delta	−0.3968	−0.8487	0
B	18.441	34.634	0
put premium	2.5687	4.8243	0
value of early exercise	0	4.8762	0

Question 10.14.

a)   We can calculate the price of the call currency option in a very similar way to our previous calculations. We simply replace the dividend yield with the foreign interest rate in our formulas. Thus, we have:

	node uu	node $ud = du$	node dd
delta	0.9925	0.9925	0.1964
B	−0.8415	−0.8415	−0.1314
call premium	0.4734	0.1446	0.0150

Using these call premia at all previous nodes yields:

	$t = 0$	node d	node u
delta	0.7038	0.5181	0.9851
B	−0.5232	−0.3703	−0.8332
call premium	0.1243	0.0587	0.2544

The price of the European call option is $0.1243.

b)   For the American call option, the binomial approach yields:

	node uu	node $ud = du$	node dd
delta	0.9925	0.9925	0.1964
B	−0.8415	−0.8415	−0.1314
call premium	0.4734	0.1446	0.0150
value of early exercise	0.4748	0.1436	0

Using the maximum of the call premium and the value of early exercise at the previous nodes and at the initial node yields:

	$t = 0$	node d	node u
delta	0.7056	0.5181	0.9894
B	−0.5247	−0.3703	−0.8374
call premium	0.1245	0.0587	0.2549
value of early exercise	0.07	0	0.2540

The price of the American call option is: $0.1245.

Question 10.16.

aa)   We now have to inverse the interest rates: We have a Yen-denominated option, therefore, the dollar interest rate becomes the foreign interest rate. With these changes, and equipped with an exchange rate of Y120/$ and a strike of Y120, we can proceed with our standard binomial procedure.

	node uu	node $ud = du$	node dd
delta	0.9835	0.1585	0
B	−119.6007	−17.4839	0
call premium	9.3756	1.0391	0

Using these call premia at all previous nodes yields:

	$t = 0$	node d	node u
delta	0.3283	0.0802	0.5733
B	−36.6885	−8.4614	−66.8456
call premium	2.7116	0.5029	5.0702

The price of the European Yen-denominated call option is $2.7116.

ab)   For the American call option, the binomial approach yields:

	node uu	node $ud = du$	node dd
delta	0.9835	0.1585	0
B	−119.6007	−17.4839	0
call premium	9.3756	1.0391	0
value of early exercise	11.1439	0	0

Using the maximum of the call premium and the value of early exercise at the previous nodes and at the initial node yields:

	$t = 0$	node d	node u
delta	0.3899	0.0802	0.6949
B	−43.6568	−8.4614	−81.2441
call premium	3.1257	0.5029	5.9259
value of early exercise	0	0	5.4483

b)   For the Yen-denominated put option, we have:

	node uu	node $ud = du$	node dd
delta	0	−0.8249	−0.9835
B	0	102.1168	119.6007
put premium	0	5.7287	17.2210
value of early exercise	0	3.1577	15.8997

We can clearly see that early exercise is never optimal at those stages. We can therefore calculate at the previous nodes:

	$t = 0$	node d	node u
delta	−0.6229	−0.8870	−0.3939
B	82.1175	110.7413	52.3571
put premium	7.37	11.602	2.9372
value of early exercise	0	8.2322	0

We can see that the American and the European put option must have the same price, since it is never optimal to exercise the American put option early. The price of the put option is 7.37.

c)   The benefit of early exercise for a put option is to receive the strike price earlier on and start earning interest on it. The cost associated with early exercising a put is to stop earning income on the asset we give up. In this case, the strike is 120 Yen, and the Yen interest rate is not very favorable compared to the dollar interest rate. We would give up a high yield instrument and receive a low yield instrument when we early exercise the put option. This is not beneficial, and it is reflected by the non-optimality of early exercise of the put option.

For the call option, the opposite is true: When exercising the call option, we receive a dollar and give up 120 Yen. Therefore, we receive the high-yield instrument, and if the exchange rate moves in our favor, we want to exercise the option before expiration.

Question 10.18.

a)   We have to use the formulas of the textbook to calculate the stock tree and the prices of the options. Remember that while it is possible to calculate a delta, the option price is just the value of B, because it does not cost anything to enter into a futures contract. In particular, this yields the following prices: For the European call and put, we have: $premium = 122.9537$. The prices must be equal due to put-call-parity.

b)   We can calculate for the American call option: $premium = 124.3347$ and for the American put option: $premium = 124.3347$.

c)   We have the following time 0 replicating portfolios:
For the European call option:

> Buy 0.5371 futures contracts.
> Borrow 122.9537

For the European put option:

> Sell 0.4141 futures contracts.
> Borrow 122.9537

Question 10.20.

a)   The price of an American call option with a strike of 95 is $24.1650.

b)   The price of an American put option with a strike of 95 is $15.2593

c)   Now, we have for the American 100-strike call option a premium of $15.2593 and for the European put option a premium of $24.165. Both option prices increase as we would have expected, and the relation we observed in question 10.19. continues to hold.

Chapter 11
Binomial Option Pricing: II

Question 11.2.

By introducing a non-zero interest rate, we increase the cost of early exercise, because we pay the strike before expiration, and lose interest on it. We see that we only exercise the call with a strike of 70. The value of the European 70-strike call is $27.69, the value of immediate exercise is $30.

The decisive condition, derived from put-call-parity, is now:

$$C = Se^{-\delta} - Ke^{-r} + P = 100 \times 0.92311 - K \times 0.92311 + P = 92.31164 - 0.92311K + P$$

Therefore, we will exercise whenever

$$100 - K > 92.31164 - 0.92311K + P$$
$$\Leftrightarrow \quad P < 7.688 - 0.07688K$$

This condition is indeed fulfilled at a strike price of 70. Clearly, this boundary is attained earlier than the boundary of exercise 11.1., so we will stop early exercise at lower strike prices when the interest rates are high.

Question 11.4.

a)   Early exercise occurs only at a strike price of 130. The value of the one period binomial European 130 strike put is $26.38, while the value of immediate exercise is $130 - 100 = 30$.

b)   From put-call-parity, we observe the following:

$$P = Ke^{-r} - Se^{-\delta} + C = K \times 0.9231164 - S + C = 92.31164K - S + C$$

Clearly, as long as $K - 100$ is larger than $92.31164K - 100 + C$ or $C < 0.07688K$, we will exercise the option early. Already at a strike of 120, $0.07688 * 120 = 9.2256$ is smaller than the value of the European call option with a strike of 120 (with a price of $10.30), which means that we do not exercise prior to expiration.

c)   The value of a call falls when the strike price increases. From part b), we learned that the decisive criterion was that $C < 0.07688K$. Therefore, if this criterion is fulfilled for some threshold $K(*)$, it is fulfilled for every K above $K(*)$.

Question 11.6.

We now have from put-call-parity:

$$P = Ke^{-r} - Se^{-\delta} + C = K - S \times 0.92311 + C = 0.92311K - 92.31164 + C$$

We would exercise early if:

$$K - 100 > K - 92.31164 + C$$
$$\Leftrightarrow \quad C < -7.688,$$

which can never be true. It is never optimal to early exercise, because the sole advantage of early exercise, receiving the interest on the strike earlier, has been removed.

Question 11.8.

For the following questions, we will report the first two of the 10 nodes. We have for the European call options of strike 70, 80, 90 and 100:

Delta and B:

	$K = 70$		$K = 80$		$K = 90$		$K = 100$
	0.98		0.94		0.88		0.77
	−62.84		−66.81		−68.35		−63.16
0.95		0.88		0.79		0.66	
−58.76		−59.44		−57.40		−50.19	
	0.91		0.81		0.68		0.54
	−55.96		−53.66		−48.32		−39.16

Call option price and gamma, the required rate of return:

	$K = 70$		$K = 80$		$K = 90$		$K = 100$
	110.83		110.83		110.83		110.83
	45.95		37.38		29.21		22.73
100.00	0.24	100.00	0.27	100.00	0.31	100.00	0.34
36.14		28.34		21.16		15.96	
0.26	91.68	0.30	91.68	0.34	91.68	0.376	91.68
	27.77		20.56		14.17		10.06
	0.29		0.33		0.39		0.42

Delta and B:

	K = 110		K = 120		K = 130
	0.67		0.55		0.43
	−57.32		−48.16		−39.00
0.54		0.43		0.31	
−42.79		−34.46		−26.13	
	0.40		0.29		0.19
	−30.24		−22.54		−14.83

Call option price and gamma:

	K = 110		K = 120		K = 130
	110.83		110.83		110.83
	16.63		12.52		8.41
100.00	0.39	100.00	0.41	100.00	0.47
11.14		8.18		5.22	
0.41	91.68	0.44	91.68	0.49	91.68
	6.30		4.36		2.41
	0.48		0.50		0.57

We clearly see that the more the option is out-of-the-money, the higher the required expected return is. This is a consequence of the option becoming more and more leveraged as it moves out of the money.

Question 11.10.

For the following questions, we will, due to space limitations, only report the first two of the 10 nodes. We have for the European put options of strike 70, 80, 90 and 100:

Delta and B:

	K = 70		K = 80		K = 90		K = 100
	−0.02		−0.06		−0.12		−0.23
	2.29		7.63		15.40		29.89
−0.05		−0.12		−0.21		−0.34	
5.85		14.41		25.68		42.12	
	−0.09		−0.19		−0.32		−0.46
	9.18		20.79		35.43		53.90

Put option price and gamma, the required rate of return:

	K = 70		K = 80		K = 90		K = 100
	110.83		110.83		110.83		110.83
	0.25		0.99		2.13		4.94
100.00	−0.51	100.00	−0.41	100.00	−0.37	100.00	−0.28
	0.75		2.19		4.24		8.27
−0.41	91.68	−0.32	91.68	−0.28	91.68	−0.21	91.68
	1.23		3.32		6.23		11.43
	−0.39		−0.30		−0.25		−0.18

Delta and B:

	K = 110		K = 120		K = 130
	−0.33		−0.45		−0.57
	45.04		63.51		81.97
−0.46		−0.57		−0.69	
58.75		76.31		93.87	
	−0.60		−0.71		−0.81
	72.12		89.13		106.14

Call option price and gamma:

	K = 110		K = 120		K = 130
	110.83		110.83		110.83
	8.16		13.35		18.55
100.00	−0.24	100.00	−0.19	100.00	−0.16
	12.68		18.95		25.23
−0.18	91.68	−0.13	91.68	−0.11	91.68
	16.98		24.34		31.69
	−0.15		−0.11		−0.09

We clearly see that the more the put option is out-of-the-money, the lower the required expected return is.

Question 11.12.

For $n = 3$, u and d are calculated as follows:

$$u = e^{(r-\delta)h+\sigma\sqrt{h}} = e^{(0.08)\times 1/3+0.3\times\sqrt{1/3}} = 1.2212$$

$$d = e^{(r-\delta)h-\sigma\sqrt{h}} = e^{(0.08)\times 1/3-0.3\times\sqrt{1/3}} = 0.8637$$

Now we can calculate $p^* = \dfrac{e^{(r-\delta)h} - d}{u - d} = 0.4568$

$n - i$	Stock price	Probability
0	182.141786	0.09532291
1	128.814742	0.34004825
2	91.1006651	0.40435476
3	64.4284267	0.16027409

The figure looks like:

Risk-neutral distribution of 1-year stock prices for n = 3

for $n = 10$, we have:

$$u = e^{(r-\delta)h + \sigma\sqrt{h}} = e^{(0.08)\times 1/10 + 0.3 \times \sqrt{1/10}} = 1.1083$$

$$d = e^{(r-\delta)h - \sigma\sqrt{h}} = e^{(0.08)\times 1/10 - 0.3 \times \sqrt{1/10}} = 0.9168$$

Now we can calculate $p^* = \dfrac{e^{(r-\delta)h} - d}{u - d} = 0.4763$

$n - i$	Stock price	Probability
0	279.738009	0.00060091
1	231.392829	0.00660713
2	191.402811	0.03269085
3	158.32399	0.0958508
4	130.961953	0.18443127
5	108.328707	0.24334174
6	89.6070076	0.22296472
7	74.1208498	0.14008734
8	61.3110573	0.0577605
9	50.7150924	0.014113
10	41.9503547	0.00155174

The figure looks like:

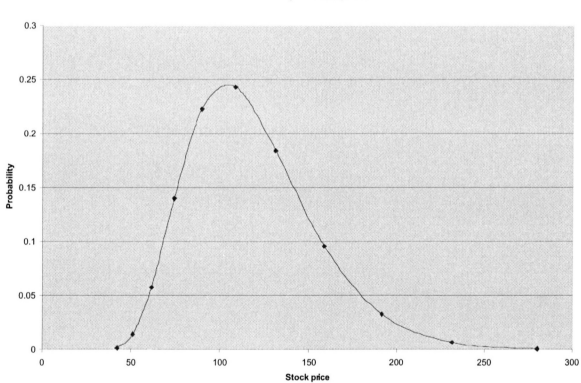

Question 11.14.

a)   We can calculate the forward prices as:

$$F_{0,4\ months} = 100e^{0.08 \times 1/3} = 102.7025$$

$$F_{0,8\ months} = 100e^{0.08 \times 2/3} = 105.4781$$

$$F_{0,1\ year} = 100e^{0.08} = 108.3287$$

b)   After $t = 1/3$ years, we have:

Stock price	Probability
122.124611	0.45680665
86.3692561	0.54319335

This yields an expectation of 102.70254, equivalent to the forward price of part a).
After $t = 2/3$ years, we have:

Stock price	Probability
149.144206	0.20867232
105.478118	0.49626867
74.596484	0.29505901

This yields an expectation of 105.4781, equivalent to the forward price of part a).
After 1 year, we have:

Stock price	Probability
182.141781	0.0953229
128.814741	0.34004825
91.1006658	0.40435476
64.4284283	0.16027409

This yields an expectation of 108.3287, equivalent to the forward price of part a).

Question 11.16.

Stock Tree

								233.621
							210.110	
						188.966		188.966
					169.949		169.949	
				152.847		152.847		152.847
			137.465		137.465		137.465	
		123.631		123.631		123.631		123.631
	111.190		111.190		111.190		111.190	
100.000		95.000		100.000		100.000		100.000
	89.937		89.937		89.937		89.937	
		80.886		80.886		80.886		80.886
			72.746		72.746		72.746	
				65.425		65.425		65.425
					58.841		58.841	
						52.920		52.920
							47.594	
								42.804

European Call

								138.621
							114.746	
						93.500		93.966
					74.600		74.836	
				57.798		57.829		57.847
			43.327		42.719		42.554	
		31.432		30.213		28.976		28.631
	22.118		20.571		18.736		16.442	
15.140		13.563		11.670		9.221		5.000
	8.703		7.065		5.080		2.431	
		4.183		2.760		1.182		0.000
			1.483		0.575		0.000	
				0.280		0.000		0.000
					0.000		0.000	
						0.000		0.000
							0.000	
								0.000

American Call

t0	t1	t2	t3	t4	t5	t6	t7	t8
								138.621
							115.110	
						93.966		93.966
					74.949		74.949	
				57.981		57.884		57.847
			43.422		42.746		42.554	
		31.482		30.226		28.976		28.631
	22.144		20.578		18.736		16.442	
15.153		13.566		11.670		9.221		5.000
	8.704		7.065		5.080		2.431	
		4.183		2.760		1.182		0.000
			1.483		0.575		0.000	
				0.280		0.000		0.000
					0.000		0.000	
						0.000		0.000
							0.000	
								0.000

European Put

t0	t1	t2	t3	t4	t5	t6	t7	t8
								0.000
							0.000	
						0.000		0.000
					0.000		0.000	
				0.458		0.000		0.000
			1.819		0.909		0.000	
		4.265		3.169		1.804		0.000
7.713		6.711		5.414		3.582		0.000
	11.194		10.263		9.006		7.110	
		15.742		15.146		14.420		14.114
			21.342		21.373		21.762	
				27.745		28.506		29.575
					34.444		35.580	
						40.857		42.080
							46.757	
								52.196

American Put

								0.000
							0.000	
						0.000		0.000
					0.000		0.000	
				0.000		0.000		0.000
			0.458		0.000		0.000	
		1.835		0.909		0.000		0.000
	4.353		3.201		1.804		0.000	
7.979		6.870		5.477		3.582		0.000
	11.637		10.548		9.131		7.110	
		16.468		15.651		14.668		14.114
			22.509		22.254		22.254	
				29.575		29.575		29.575
					36.159		36.159	
						42.080		42.080
							47.406	
								52.196

Question 11.18.

We chose the stock of IBM from June 1st 1997 to May 31st 2002 (http://finance.yahoo.com). Please note that we must calculate the continuously compounded returns before we can calculate the weekly standard deviation. (c.f. table 11.1 of the textbook). We obtain the annual standard deviation by multiplying our weekly estimate by the square root of 52.

In particular, this yields:

Period	Weekly	Annual
97/6 – 02/05	0.050	0.360
97/6 – 98/5	0.040	0.287
98/6 – 99/5	0.049	0.355
99/6 – 00/5	0.052	0.376
00/6 – 01/5	0.063	0.457
01/6 – 02/5	0.040	0.287
97/6 – 97/11	0.039	0.279
97/12 – 98/5	0.041	0.298
98/6 – 98/11	0.043	0.311
98/12 – 99/5	0.056	0.401
99/6 – 99/11	0.055	0.395
99/12 – 00/5	0.050	0.364
00/6 – 00/11	0.060	0.432
00/12 – 01/5	0.067	0.486
01/6 – 01/11	0.037	0.268
01/12 – 02/5	0.041	0.297

We can observe a time trend in the volatility estimate: Volatility is rising throughout the nineties, up to a record level of over 45 percent in 2000/2001. Only the last year of data shows a reversal in the volatility.

There does not seem to be an additional pattern to be detected when we conduct the semiannual volatility estimates.

Question 11.20.

We will use the methodology introduced by Hull, which is described in the main textbook. We can calculate:

$$u = 1.2005 \quad S = 50.0000 \quad K = 45.00$$
$$d = 0.8670 \quad F = 46.0792 \quad \text{dividend} = 4.0000$$
$$p = 0.4594 \quad t = 1.0000 \quad r = 0.0800$$
$$n = 4.0000 \quad h = 0.2500 \quad \text{sigma} = 0.3255$$
$$\text{time to div } 0.2500$$

American Call

					95.7188
					50.7188
				79.7304	
				35.6215	
			66.4127		69.1230
			23.1772		24.1230
		59.3195		57.5771	
		14.3195		13.4682	
	50.0000		47.9597		49.9170
	8.4551		7.2380		4.9170
		43.3480		41.5791	
		3.7876		2.2141	
			34.6340		36.0474
			0.9970		0.0000
				30.0263	
				0.0000	
					26.0315
					0.0000

European
Call

					95.7188
					50.7188
				79.7304	
				35.6215	
			66.4127		69.1230
			23.1772		24.1230
		59.3195		57.5771	
		14.2721		13.4682	
	50.0000		47.9597		49.9170
	8.4338		7.2380		4.9170
		43.3480		41.5791	
		3.7876		2.2141	
			34.6340		36.0474
			0.9970		0.0000
				30.0263	
				0.0000	
					26.0315
					0.0000

Chapter 12
The Black-Scholes Formula

Question 12.2.

N	Call	Put
8	3.464	1.718
9	3.361	1.642
10	3.454	1.711
11	3.348	1.629
12	3.446	1.705

The observed values are slowly converging towards the Black-Scholes values of the example. Please note that the binomial solution oscillates as it approaches the Black-Scholes value.

Question 12.4.

a)

T	Call Price
1	18.6705
2	18.1410
5	15.1037
10	10.1571
50	0.2938
100	0.0034
500	0.0000

The benefit to holding the call option is that we do not have to pay the strike price and that we continue to earn interest on the strike. On the other hand, the owner of the call option foregoes the dividend payments he could receive if he owned the stock. As the interest rate is zero and the dividend yield is positive, the cost of holding the call outweighs the benefits.

b)

T	Call Price
1	18.7281
2	18.2284
5	15.2313
10	10.2878
50	0.3045
100	0.0036
500	0.0000

Although the call option is worth marginally more when we introduce the interest rate of 0.001, it is still not enough to outweigh the cost of not receiving the huge dividend yield.

Question 12.6.

a)   Using the Black-Scholes formula, we find a call-price of $16.33.

b)   We determine the one year forward price to be:

$$F_{0,T}(S) = S * \exp(r * T) = \$100 * \exp(0.06 * 1) = \$106.1837$$

c)   As the textbook suggests, we need to set the dividend yield equal to the risk-free rate when using the Black-Scholes formula. Thus:

$$C(106.1837, 105, 0.4, 0.06, 1, \mathbf{0.06}) = \$16.33$$

This exercise shows the general result that a European futures option has the same value as the European stock option provided the futures contract has the same expiration as the stock option.

Question 12.8.

a)   We have to be careful here: Now we have to take into account the dividend yield when calculating the 9-month forward price:

$$F_{0,T}(S) = S * \exp((r - \text{delta}) * T) = \$100 * \exp((0.08 - 0.03) * 0.75) = \$103.8212.$$

b)   Having found the correct forward price, we can use equation (12.7) to price the call option on the futures contract: $C(103.8212, 95, 0.3, 0.08, 0.75, \mathbf{0.08}) = \$14.3863$

c)   The price we found in part b) and the prices of the previous question are identical. 12.7a, 12.7b and 12.8b are all based on the same Black-Scholes formula, only the way in which we input the variables differs.

Question 12.10.

Time decay is measured by the greek letter theta. We will show in the following that the statement of the exercise is not always correct.

We assume $S = 50$, sigma $= 0.3$, $r = 0.08$, delta $= 0$, $K = 40$, 50 and 60, and $T = 1$ month, 3 months, ... , 13 months.

We can calculate:

K = 40

Time to expiration	Theta	Call price	Dollar change	Perc. change
1 month	−0.010	10.271	−0.010	−0.09%
3 months	−0.012	10.939	−0.012	−0.11%
5 months	−0.012	11.678	−0.012	−0.11%
7 months	−0.012	12.409	−0.012	−0.10%
9 months	−0.012	13.115	−0.012	−0.09%
11 months	−0.011	13.792	−0.011	−0.08%
13 months	−0.011	14.443	−0.011	−0.07%

K = 50

	Theta	Call price	Dollar change	Perc. change
1 month	−0.034	1.892	−0.034	−1.82%
3 months	−0.022	3.481	−0.022	−0.63%
5 months	−0.018	4.669	−0.018	−0.39%
7 months	−0.016	5.688	−0.016	−0.28%
9 months	−0.015	6.606	−0.015	−0.22%
11 months	−0.014	7.453	−0.014	−0.18%
13 months	−0.013	8.247	−0.013	−0.16%

K = 60

	Theta	Call price	Dollar change	Perc. change
1 month	−0.004	0.037	−0.004	−11.14%
3 months	−0.012	0.577	−0.012	−2.01%
5 months	−0.013	1.319	−0.013	−0.97%
7 months	−0.013	2.088	−0.013	−0.61%
9 months	−0.012	2.846	−0.012	−0.44%
11 months	−0.012	3.586	−0.012	−0.34%
13 months	−0.012	4.306	−0.012	−0.27%

Please note that we measure theta as the dollar change in the call value per day. Therefore, we divided the returned value of the Excel function BSTheta by 360.

We can see that in fact the statement of the exercise is not correct. Only the at the money call option ($K = 50$) has a monotonically decreasing theta (in time) and thus the greatest time decay for short expirations (i.e., a decreasing dollar and percentage price change if we reduce the time to maturity by one day). Both the out of the money and in the money option have thetas that are not monotonically decreasing in time to maturity, and neither the dollar change nor the percentage change are necessarily greater the shorter the time to expiration is.

In the money and out of the money options can have thetas that are increasing in time to maturity, as the following figure, graphing the theta of the above options, depending on time to maturity, shows:

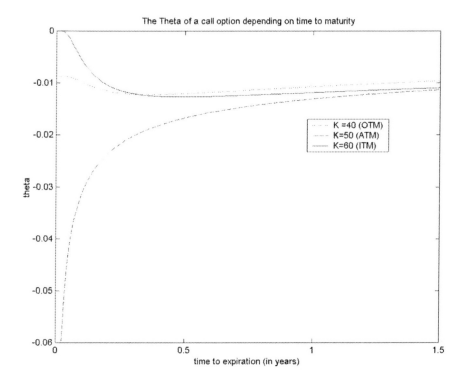

Question 12.12.

epsilon	call_u	call_d	div_appr.
0.0010	14.3364	14.4363	−0.4997
0.0100	13.8923	14.8917	−0.4997
0.1000	9.9457	19.9526	−0.5003

Let's do a quick check: $C(\ldots, \text{delta} = 0.03) = 14.3863$, $C(\ldots, \text{delta} = 0.04) = 13.8923$. The difference is -0.4940, which is very close to our approximation of -0.4997.

Question 12.14.

a)   The greeks of the bull spread are simply the sum of the greeks of the individual options. The greeks of the call with a strike of 45 enter with a negative sign because this option was sold.

	Bought Call(40)	Sold Call(45)	Bull Spread
Price	4.1553	−2.1304	2.0249
Delta	0.6159	−0.3972	0.2187
Gamma	0.0450	−0.0454	−0.0004
Vega	0.1081	−0.1091	−0.0010
Theta	−0.0136	0.0121	−0.0014
Rho	0.1024	−0.0688	0.0336

b)

	Bought Call(40)	Sold Call(45)	Bull Spread
Price	7.7342	−4.6747	3.0596
Delta	0.8023	−0.6159	0.1864
Gamma	0.0291	−0.0400	−0.0109
Vega	0.0885	−0.0122	−0.0331
Theta	−0.0137	0.0152	0.0016
Rho	0.1418	−0.1152	0.0267

c)   Because we simultaneously buy and sell an option, the graphs of gamma, vega and theta have inflection points (see figures below). Therefore, the initial intuition one may have had—that the greeks should be symmetric at $S = \$40$ and $S = \$45$—is not correct.

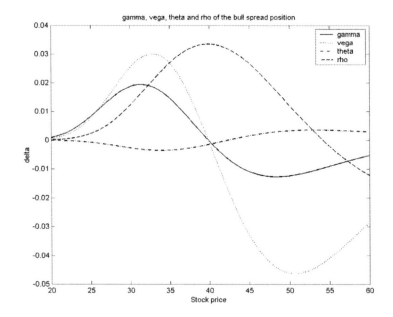

Question 12.16.

a)   1 day to expiration

S	call delta	put delta	call vega	put vega	call theta	put theta	call rho	put rho
60	0.000	−1.000	0.000	0.000	0.000	0.022	0.000	−0.003
65	0.000	−1.000	0.000	0.000	0.000	0.022	0.000	−0.003
70	0.000	−1.000	0.000	0.000	0.000	0.022	0.000	−0.003
75	0.000	−1.000	0.000	0.000	0.000	0.022	0.000	−0.003
80	0.000	−1.000	0.000	0.000	0.000	0.022	0.000	−0.003
85	0.000	−1.000	0.000	0.000	0.000	0.022	0.000	−0.003
90	0.000	−1.000	0.000	0.000	0.000	0.022	0.000	−0.003
95	0.001	−0.999	0.000	0.000	−0.002	0.021	0.000	−0.003
100	0.509	−0.491	0.021	0.021	−0.326	−0.304	0.001	−0.001
105	0.999	−0.001	0.000	0.000	−0.025	−0.003	0.003	0.000
110	1.000	0.000	0.000	0.000	−0.022	0.000	0.003	0.000
115	1.000	0.000	0.000	0.000	−0.022	0.000	0.003	0.000
120	1.000	0.000	0.000	0.000	−0.022	0.000	0.003	0.000
125	1.000	0.000	0.000	0.000	−0.022	0.000	0.003	0.000
130	1.000	0.000	0.000	0.000	−0.022	0.000	0.003	0.000
135	1.000	0.000	0.000	0.000	−0.022	0.000	0.003	0.000
140	1.000	0.000	0.000	0.000	−0.022	0.000	0.003	0.000

ab)   1 year to expiration

S	call delta	put delta	call vega	put vega	call theta	put theta	call rho	put rho
60	0.099	−0.901	0.105	0.105	−0.006	0.015	0.052	−0.871
65	0.154	−0.846	0.154	0.154	−0.008	0.012	0.086	−0.837
70	0.220	−0.780	0.207	0.207	−0.012	0.009	0.131	−0.792
75	0.294	−0.706	0.258	0.258	−0.015	0.006	0.184	−0.739
80	0.372	−0.628	0.303	0.303	−0.018	0.002	0.245	−0.678
85	0.450	−0.550	0.336	0.336	−0.021	0.000	0.310	−0.614
90	0.526	−0.474	0.358	0.358	−0.023	−0.003	0.376	−0.547
95	0.597	−0.403	0.368	0.368	−0.025	−0.005	0.442	−0.482
100	0.662	−0.338	0.366	0.366	−0.026	−0.006	0.504	−0.419
105	0.719	−0.281	0.354	0.354	−0.027	−0.007	0.563	−0.360
110	0.769	−0.231	0.335	0.335	−0.028	−0.007	0.617	−0.306
115	0.811	−0.189	0.311	0.311	−0.028	−0.007	0.665	−0.259
120	0.847	−0.153	0.283	0.283	−0.028	−0.007	0.707	−0.216
125	0.877	−0.123	0.254	0.254	−0.027	−0.007	0.743	−0.180
130	0.902	−0.098	0.225	0.225	−0.027	−0.006	0.775	−0.148
135	0.922	−0.078	0.197	0.197	−0.026	−0.006	0.801	−0.122
140	0.938	−0.062	0.171	0.171	−0.025	−0.005	0.824	−0.100

We can clearly see that the entries for the one day expiration table are more extreme: There is only one day left for stock price changes, so a lot of uncertainty is resolved. For example, a deep out of the money call option (e.g. at a stock price of $60) is unlikely to change during one day to some price bigger than $100, so the option most likely does not pay off, therefore its delta is zero. On the other hand, with one year to maturity left, there is a decent chance of such a change, therefore the price of the option reacts to a one dollar increase in the stock price.

ba)   Time to expiration: 1 day

S	straddle delta	straddle vega	straddle theta	straddle rho
60	−1.000	0.000	0.022	−0.003
65	−1.000	0.000	0.022	−0.003
70	−1.000	0.000	0.022	−0.003
75	−1.000	0.000	0.022	−0.003
80	−1.000	0.000	0.022	−0.003
85	−1.000	0.000	0.022	−0.003
90	−1.000	0.000	0.022	−0.003
95	−0.999	0.000	0.019	−0.003
100	0.018	0.042	−0.631	0.000
105	0.998	0.000	−0.027	0.003
110	1.000	0.000	−0.022	0.003
115	1.000	0.000	−0.022	0.003
120	1.000	0.000	−0.022	0.003
125	1.000	0.000	−0.022	0.003
130	1.000	0.000	−0.022	0.003
135	1.000	0.000	−0.022	0.003
140	1.000	0.000	−0.022	0.003

bb)   Time to expiration: 1 year

S	straddle delta	straddle vega	straddle theta	straddle rho
60	−0.802	0.209	0.009	−0.819
65	−0.692	0.308	0.004	−0.750
70	−0.560	0.415	−0.003	−0.661
75	−0.412	0.517	−0.009	−0.554
80	−0.256	0.605	−0.016	−0.433
85	−0.100	0.673	−0.021	−0.304
90	0.052	0.717	−0.026	−0.171
95	0.194	0.735	−0.030	−0.040
100	0.323	0.732	−0.032	0.086
105	0.438	0.708	−0.034	0.203
110	0.537	0.670	−0.035	0.310
115	0.623	0.622	−0.035	0.406
120	0.694	0.567	−0.035	0.490
125	0.754	0.509	−0.034	0.564
130	0.803	0.451	−0.033	0.626
135	0.844	0.395	−0.032	0.679
140	0.876	0.342	−0.030	0.724

bc)   Explanation of the one year greeks

We need to keep in mind that we bought a call option and bought a put option, both with a strike of $100. Therefore, with a stock price smaller than $100, the put option is in the money, and the call option is out of the money. This pattern helps us when we look at the greeks: For small stock prices, delta is negative (the put dominates) and rho is negative (recall that since the put entitles the owner to receive cash, and the present value of this is lower with a higher interest rate, the rho of a put is negative). Deep in the money put options have a positive theta, therefore for very small stock prices, we expect (and see) a positive theta of the straddle. However, once we increase the stock price, the theta of a put becomes negative; the theta becomes progressively more negative as the negative theta effects of the call are integrated. Both put and call have the same vega, and we know that vega is highest for at the money options.

ca)

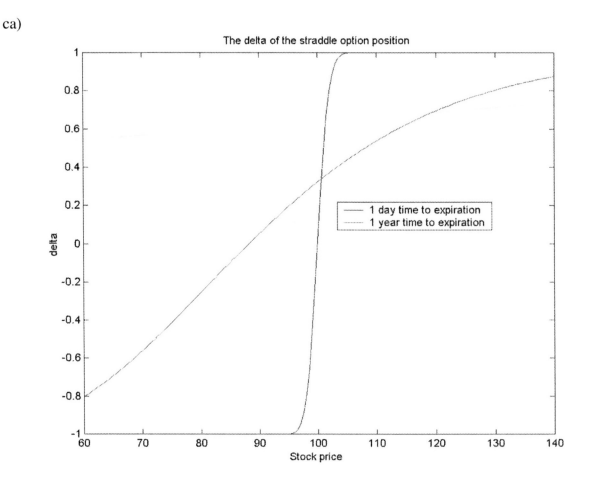

The delta of the one day time to expiration graph is a lot steeper. However, delta changes only in a small area around the strike price. With only one day to expiration left, it becomes increasingly clear whether the call option ends out of the money (delta_c = 0) and the put option ends in the money (delta_p = −1) or the call option in the money (delta_c = 1) and the put option out of the money (delta_p = 0). Taken together, this yields a delta of the straddle of either −1 or 1.

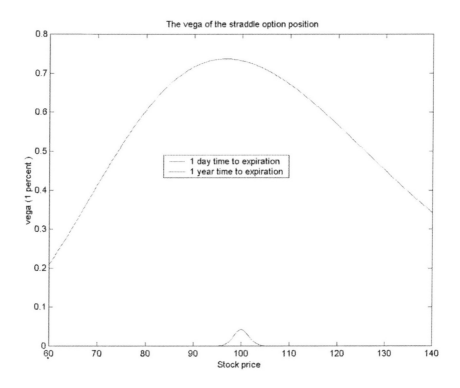

cb)   Vega:

The one-day time to expiration vega graph shows only a small hump around the strike price of the option position. With only one day time to expiration left, we do not have enough time to participate in the opportunities the one percentage point increase in volatility offers to our bought straddle. However, with one year left, we see that the volatility increase has a huge effect on our straddle.

cc)   Theta:

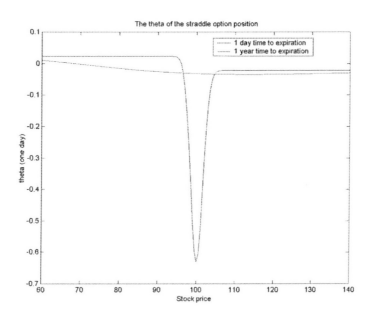

Remember, we bought a call and a put option on the same strike of $100. This figure is a nice demonstration that for bought at the money option positions, time decay is greatest for short time to maturity positions. Our long straddle will pay off if either the call or the put is in the money. If the current stock price is about 100 and we have only one day to expiration left, our option position will likely expire worthless. Therefore, there is a huge time decay. With longer time to maturities, chances of stock price movements away from a 100 are substantial. Therefore, the theta is much smoother and smaller.

cd) rho:

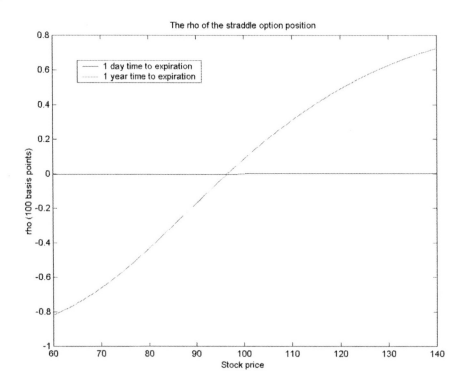

With one day to maturity left, a 100 basis point increase in the interest rate has no effect on the option position, because the time we could earn interest/lose interest on the strike is just too short.

For the one year to maturity figure, we can see the following: If the stock price is higher than $100, it is the call option that is in the money, and the put expires worthless. Therefore, rho is positive (remember, rho for a call option is positive, because a call entails paying the fixed strike price to receive the stock and a higher interest rate reduces the present value of the strike). For stock prices smaller than $100, the put dominates and we know that the rho of a put is negative.

Tables for 12.18.

Inputs			Perpetual Options	
			Call	**Put**
Stock price	50			
Exercise price	60	Option Price	26.35183	23.07471
Volatility	40.000%	Exercise at:	317.3092	22.6908
Risk-free interest rate	6.000%			
Dividend yield	3.000%			

Inputs			Perpetual Options	
			Call	**Put**
Stock price	50			
Exercise price	60	Option Price	22.75128	23.82482
Volatility	40.000%	Exercise at:	248.2475	21.75248
Risk-free interest rate	6.000%			
Dividend yield	4.000%			

Inputs			Perpetual Options	
			Call	**Put**
Stock price	50			
Exercise price	60	Option Price	27.10008	21.2744
Volatility	40.000%	Exercise at:	334.9193	25.08067
Risk-free interest rate	7.000%			
Dividend yield	3.000%			

Inputs			Perpetual Options	
			Call	**Put**
Stock price	50			
Exercise price	60	Option Price	29.83555	27.62938
Volatility	50.000%	Exercise at:	412.5475	17.45254
Risk-free interest rate	6.000%			
Dividend yield	3.000%			

Question 12.18.

a) The price of the perpetual call option is $26.35. It should be exercised when the stock price reaches the barrier of $317.31.

b) The price of the perpetual call option is now $22.75. It should be exercised when the stock price reaches the barrier of $248.25. The higher dividend yield makes it more costly to forego the dividends and wait for an increase in the stock price before exercising the option. Therefore, the option is worth less and it is optimal to exercise after a smaller increase in the underlying stock price.

c) The price of the perpetual call option is now $27.10. It should be exercised when the stock price reaches the barrier of $334.92. The higher interest rate increases the value of the call option and makes it attractive to wait a bit longer before you exercise the option, as you can continue to earn interest on the strike before you exercise. Therefore, the option is worth more and it is only optimal to exercise after a larger increase in the underlying stock price.

d)   The price of the perpetual call option is $29.84. It should be exercised when the stock price reaches the barrier of $412.55. Options love volatility. The chances of an even larger increase in the stock price are high with a large standard deviation (and your risk is capped at the downside). Therefore, the option is worth more and you wait longer until you forego the future potential and exercise.

Question 12.20.

a) $C(100, 90, 0.3, 0.08, 1, 0.05) = 17.6988$

b) $P(90, 100, 0.3, 0.05, 1, 0.08) = 17.6988$

c)   The prices are equal. This is a result of the mathematical equivalence of the pricing formulas. To see this, we need some algebra. We start from equation (12.3) of the text, the formula for the European put option:

$$P(\bullet) = \overline{K} \times \exp(-\overline{r}T) \times N\left(-\frac{\ln\left(\frac{\overline{S}}{\overline{K}}\right) + \left(\overline{r} - \overline{\delta} - 0.5\sigma^2\right)T}{\sigma\sqrt{T}}\right) - \overline{S} \times \exp(-\overline{\delta}T)$$

$$\times N\left(-\frac{\ln\left(\frac{\overline{S}}{\overline{K}}\right) + \left(\overline{r} - \overline{\delta} + 0.5\sigma^2\right)T}{\sigma\sqrt{T}}\right)$$

Now we replace:

$$\overline{K} = S, \overline{r} = \delta, \overline{\delta} = r, \overline{S} = K$$

Then:

$$= S \times \exp(-\delta T) \times N\left(-\frac{\ln\left(\frac{K}{S}\right) + \left(\delta - r - 0.5\sigma^2\right)T}{\sigma\sqrt{T}}\right) - K$$

$$\times \exp(-rT) \times N\left(-\frac{\ln\left(\frac{K}{S}\right) + \left(\delta - r + 0.5\sigma^2\right)T}{\sigma\sqrt{T}}\right)$$

Since $\ln\left(\dfrac{K}{S}\right) = -\ln\left(\dfrac{S}{K}\right)$

$$= S \times \exp\left(-\delta T\right) \times N\left(\frac{\ln\left(\frac{S}{K}\right) - \left(\delta - r - 0.5\sigma^2\right)T}{\sigma\sqrt{T}}\right) - K \times \exp\left(-rT\right)$$

$$\times N\left(\frac{\ln\left(\frac{S}{K}\right) - \left(\delta - r + 0.5\sigma^2\right)T}{\sigma\sqrt{T}}\right)$$

$$= S \times \exp\left(-\delta T\right) \times N\left(d_1\right) - K \times \exp\left(-rT\right) \times N\left(d_2\right) = C\left(\bullet\right)$$

Chapter 13
Market-Making and Delta-Hedging

Question 13.2.

Using the Black Scholes formula we can solve for the put premium and the put's delta: $P = 1.9905$ and $\Delta = -0.4176$. If we write this option, we will have a position that moves with the stock price. This implies our delta hedge will require shorting 41.76 shares (receiving $41.76\,(40) = \$1670.4$). As before, we must look at the three components of the profit. There will now be interest *earned* since we are receiving both the option premium 199.05 as well as the 1670.40 on the short sale. This $1869.43 will earn (rounding to the nearest penny) $1869.43 * e^{.08/365} - 1[1] = .41$ in interest. If the stock falls to 39 we make 41.76 on our short sale and if the stock price rises to 40.5 we lose 20.88 on our short sale. If the stock prices falls to 39 or rises to 40.5 the price of the put option we wrote will be (using $T = 90/365$) $P\,(39) = 2.4331$ or $P\,(40.5) = 1.7808$. This implies our option position will lose $243.31 - 199.05 = 44.26$ if the stock falls by \$1 and make $199.05 - 178.08 = 20.97$ if the stock rises by \$0.50. Combining these results, our profit will be

$$41.76 - 44.26 + .41 = -2.09 \tag{1}$$

if the stock price falls to \$39 and

$$-20.88 + 20.97 + .41 = .50. \tag{2}$$

Notice that, as in the case of the call option, the large change implies a loss and the small change involves a profit.

Question 13.4.

The 45-strike put has a premium of 5.0824 and a delta of -0.7185 and the 40-strike put has a premium of 1.9905 and a delta of -0.4176. For the put ratio spread (assume on 100 shares), our total cost is $508.24 - 200\,(1.9905) = 110.14$. The delta on this position is $100\,(-0.7185 - 2\,(-0.4176)) = 11.67$ hence our delta hedged requires shorting 11.67 shares (receiving $11.67\,(40) = \$466.80$). This implies that in one day we will receive $466.8\,\left(e^{.08/365} - 1\right) = 0.10232 \approx .10$ from our short sale proceeds. Our short sale of 11.67 shares will make 11.67 if S falls to 59 and will lose 5.89 if S rises to 60.5. If S falls to 39 in one day the 45-strike and 40-strike puts will be worth 5.8265 and 2.4331 (respectively). This implies our put ratio spread will be worth $582.65 - (2)\,243.31 = 96.03$ (we lose $110.14 - 96.03 = 14.11$). If S rises to 40.5 in one day the 45-strike and 40-strike puts will be worth 4.7257 and 1.7808 (respectively) which implies put ratio spread will be worth $472.57 - 2\,(178.08) = 116.41$ (we make $116.41 - 110.14 = 6.27$). Combining these three components, our profit will be

$$11.67 - 14.11 + .10 = -2.34 \tag{3}$$

if S falls to 39 and

$$-5.89 + 6.27 + .10 = .48 \tag{4}$$

if S rises to 40.5. This suggests that the put ratio spread has a negative gamma at 40.

Question 13.6.

See Table Two. Once again, note the similarities with the delta hedged call.

TABLE TWO (Problem 13.6)

Day	0	1	2	3	4	5
Stock ($)	40	40.642	40.018	39.403	38.797	39.42
Put ($)	199.05	172.66	196.53	222.60	250.87	220.07
Option Delta	-0.4176	-0.3768	-0.4173	-0.4592	-0.5020	-0.4594
Investment ($)	-1869.433	-1704.224	-1866.514	-2031.895	-2198.561	-2031.022
Interest ($)		0.41	0.37	0.41	0.45	0.48
Capital Gain ($)		-0.42	-0.35	-0.40	-0.45	-0.48
Daily Profit		-0.01	0.02	0.01	0.00	0.00

Question 13.8.

See Table Four on the next page. Note the errors are larger the farther out we go as the theta will be changing. With the one day the error is minimal at $S = 40$ due to no error due to changes in S (since it will not be changing) and little error due to our theta approximation for in doesn't change much during the day. For 5 days, there is a theta error at $S_{5/365} = 40$ (of .0003) due to theta decreasing during the five days. Note that the error of .0003 is not constant across the range of prices. Besides the familiar delta-gamma error (i.e. ignoring third order changes of S), there is the effect changes in S have on Θ (technically the cross partial derivative $\partial^2 f(S,t) / (\partial S \partial t)$). The delta gamma error is symmetric; however this cross partial error is not symmetric. To see this, we can use the fundamental theorem of calculus on the Black Scholes formula. By put call parity, the put and call will have the same second cross partial derivative which is equal to

$$\frac{\partial^2 f(S,t)}{\partial S \partial t} = -\Delta_{call} \frac{r - \sigma^2/2}{\sqrt{T-t}}. \tag{5}$$

In this case this, $r - \sigma^2/2 > 0$ and $\Delta_{call} > 0$, hence the above term is negative; this implies our approximation does not include terms like $\frac{\partial^2 f(S,t)}{\partial S \partial t}(\Delta S)(\Delta t)$ which will be positive when $S_T < 40$ and negative when $S_T > 40$; hence our approximation will underestimate the option value for low S_T and overestimate it for large S_T.

TABLE FOUR (Problem 13.8)

Future S	1 day Approx	Actual	5 days Approx	Actual	25 days Approx	Actual	Errors 1d	5d	25d
25.00	13.4458	13.5091	13.4257	13.5389	13.3256	13.6910	-0.0634	-0.1132	-0.3655
25.50	12.9188	13.0236	12.8988	13.0524	12.7986	13.2004	-0.1048	-0.1537	-0.4018
26.00	12.4032	12.5414	12.3831	12.5692	12.2830	12.7123	-0.1382	-0.1861	-0.4293
26.50	11.8989	12.0631	11.8789	12.0897	11.7787	12.2273	-0.1642	-0.2109	-0.4486
27.00	11.4059	11.5892	11.3859	11.6146	11.2857	11.7458	-0.1833	-0.2287	-0.4600
27.50	10.9243	11.1204	10.9043	11.1443	10.8041	11.2685	-0.1961	-0.2400	-0.4644
28.00	10.4541	10.6573	10.4340	10.6796	10.3339	10.7960	-0.2033	-0.2456	-0.4621
28.50	9.9951	10.2005	9.9751	10.2211	9.8749	10.3289	-0.2054	-0.2460	-0.4540
29.00	9.5475	9.7507	9.5275	9.7694	9.4273	9.8680	-0.2031	-0.2419	-0.4407
29.50	9.1113	9.3084	9.0913	9.3253	8.9911	9.4140	-0.1971	-0.2340	-0.4229
30.00	8.6864	8.8744	8.6663	8.8892	8.5662	8.9675	-0.1880	-0.2229	-0.4013
30.50	8.2728	8.4492	8.2528	8.4619	8.1526	8.5293	-0.1764	-0.2091	-0.3767
31.00	7.8706	8.0335	7.8505	8.0440	7.7504	8.1000	-0.1630	-0.1935	-0.3497
31.50	7.4797	7.6278	7.4596	7.6361	7.3595	7.6805	-0.1482	-0.1765	-0.3210
32.00	7.1001	7.2327	7.0801	7.2387	6.9799	7.2712	-0.1325	-0.1586	-0.2913
32.50	6.7319	6.8485	6.7119	6.8523	6.6117	6.8728	-0.1166	-0.1404	-0.2611
33.00	6.3750	6.4758	6.3550	6.4773	6.2548	6.4860	-0.1008	-0.1223	-0.2312
33.50	6.0295	6.1150	6.0095	6.1143	5.9093	6.1111	-0.0855	-0.1048	-0.2018
34.00	5.6953	5.7663	5.6753	5.7634	5.5751	5.7486	-0.0710	-0.0882	-0.1736
34.50	5.3724	5.4301	5.3524	5.4251	5.2522	5.3990	-0.0576	-0.0727	-0.1468
35.00	5.0609	5.1064	5.0409	5.0994	4.9407	5.0625	-0.0455	-0.0585	-0.1218
35.50	4.7607	4.7956	4.7407	4.7867	4.6405	4.7394	-0.0349	-0.0460	-0.0989
36.00	4.4719	4.4976	4.4519	4.4869	4.3517	4.4299	-0.0257	-0.0350	-0.0782
36.50	4.1944	4.2125	4.1744	4.2001	4.0742	4.1340	-0.0181	-0.0257	-0.0599
37.00	3.9282	3.9403	3.9082	3.9263	3.8080	3.8519	-0.0121	-0.0181	-0.0438
37.50	3.6734	3.6809	3.6534	3.6655	3.5532	3.5834	-0.0075	-0.0121	-0.0302
38.00	3.4299	3.4341	3.4099	3.4174	3.3097	3.3285	-0.0042	-0.0075	-0.0187
38.50	3.1978	3.1998	3.1777	3.1820	3.0776	3.0870	-0.0020	-0.0043	-0.0094
39.00	2.9770	2.9778	2.9569	2.9590	2.8568	2.8587	-0.0008	-0.0020	**-0.0019**
39.50	2.7675	2.7677	2.7475	2.7481	2.6473	2.6433	-0.0002	-0.0006	0.0040
40.00	2.5694	2.5694	2.5493	2.5490	2.4492	2.4406	**0.0000**	**0.0003**	0.0085
40.50	2.3826	2.3824	2.3626	2.3615	2.2624	2.2502	0.0002	0.0011	0.0122
41.00	2.2071	2.2064	2.1871	2.1851	2.0869	2.0717	0.0007	0.0020	0.0152
41.50	2.0430	2.0411	2.0230	2.0195	1.9228	1.9047	0.0019	0.0035	0.0181
42.00	1.8903	1.8860	1.8702	1.8643	1.7701	1.7488	0.0042	0.0060	0.0213
42.50	1.7488	1.7408	1.7288	1.7190	1.6286	1.6034	0.0080	0.0098	0.0252
43.00	1.6187	1.6051	1.5987	1.5833	1.4985	1.4682	0.0137	0.0154	0.0304
43.50	1.5000	1.4783	1.4800	1.4567	1.3798	1.3426	0.0217	0.0233	0.0372
44.00	1.3926	1.3602	1.3726	1.3388	1.2724	1.2262	0.0324	0.0338	0.0461
44.50	1.2965	1.2502	1.2765	1.2291	1.1763	1.1186	0.0463	0.0474	0.0578
45.00	1.2118	1.1480	1.1917	1.1273	1.0916	1.0191	0.0638	0.0645	0.0725
45.50	1.1384	1.0531	1.1184	1.0328	1.0182	0.9273	0.0853	0.0855	0.0908
46.00	1.0763	0.9651	1.0563	0.9454	0.9561	0.8429	0.1112	0.1109	0.1133
46.50	1.0256	0.8837	1.0056	0.8645	0.9054	0.7652	0.1420	0.1411	0.1402
47.00	0.9862	0.8084	0.9662	0.7898	0.8660	0.6940	0.1779	0.1764	0.1721
47.50	0.9582	0.7388	0.9382	0.7209	0.8380	0.6286	0.2194	0.2173	0.2094
48.00	0.9415	0.6747	0.9215	0.6574	0.8213	0.5689	0.2668	0.2640	0.2524
48.50	0.9362	0.6156	0.9161	0.5990	0.8160	0.5143	0.3205	0.3171	0.3017
49.00	0.9421	0.5612	0.9221	0.5454	0.8219	0.4644	0.3809	0.3767	0.3575
49.50	0.9595	0.5113	0.9394	0.4961	0.8393	0.4190	0.4482	0.4433	0.4203
50.00	0.9881	0.4654	0.9681	0.4509	0.8679	0.3776	0.5227	0.5172	0.4903
50.50	1.0281	0.4233	1.0081	0.4095	0.9079	0.3400	0.6048	0.5986	0.5679
51.00	1.0795	0.3847	1.0594	0.3716	0.9593	0.3059	0.6947	0.6878	0.6534
51.50	1.1421	0.3494	1.1221	0.3370	1.0219	0.2750	0.7927	0.7851	0.7470
52.00	1.2162	0.3171	1.1961	0.3054	1.0960	0.2469	0.8990	0.8907	0.8490
52.50	1.3015	0.2876	1.2815	0.2765	1.1813	0.2216	1.0139	1.0049	0.9597
53.00	1.3982	0.2607	1.3782	0.2502	1.2780	0.1986	1.1375	1.1279	1.0794
53.50	1.5062	0.2362	1.4862	0.2263	1.3860	0.1780	1.2701	1.2599	1.2081
54.00	1.6256	0.2138	1.6056	0.2045	1.5054	0.1593	1.4118	1.4011	1.3461
54.50	1.7563	0.1934	1.7363	0.1847	1.6361	0.1425	1.5629	1.5516	1.4936
55.00	1.8984	0.1749	1.8784	0.1667	1.7782	0.1274	1.7235	1.7116	1.6508

Question 13.10.

See Figures 2 & 3.

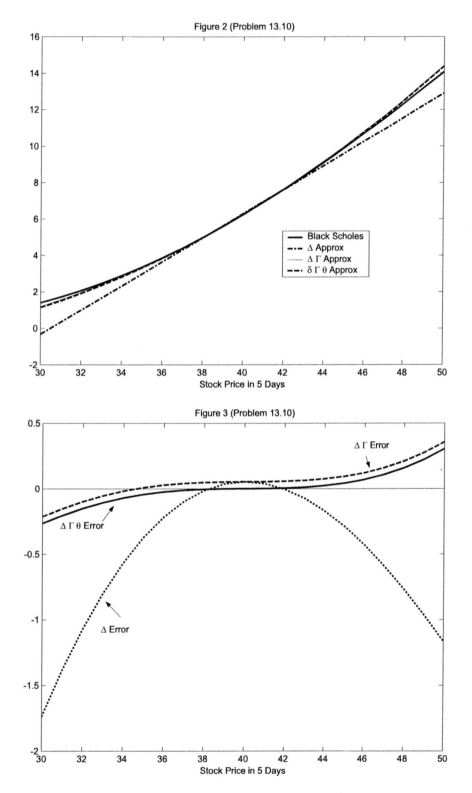

Question 13.12.

See Figures 5 & 6.

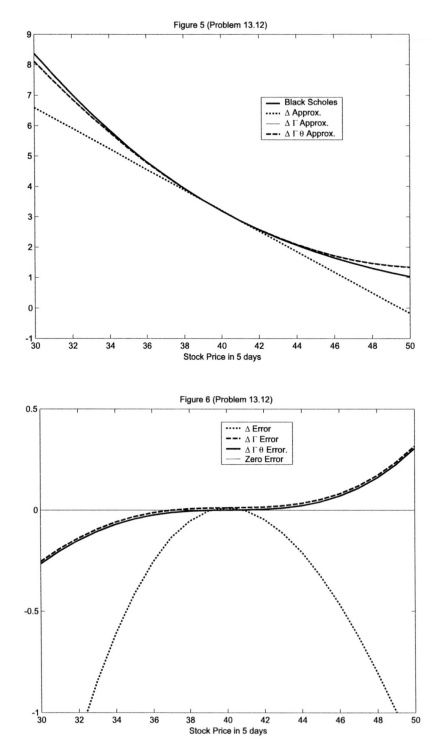

Figure 5 (Problem 13.12)

Figure 6 (Problem 13.12)

Question 13.14.

Using the given parameters, a six month 45-strike put has a price and Greeks of $P = 5.3659$, $\Delta = -.6028$, $\Gamma = .045446$, and $\Theta_{\text{per day}} = -.0025$. Note that Θ, as given in the software is a per day. Equation (13.9) uses annualized rates (i.e. Θh is in the equation. Hence for equation (13.9) we should use $-.9139$. For equation (13.9) we have a market-maker profit of

$$-\left(\frac{.09}{2} 40^2 \, (.045446) - .9139 + .08 \, ((-.6028) \, 40 - 5.3659) \right) h \tag{6}$$

$$= -(3.2721 - .9139 - 2.3582) \, h = 0. \tag{7}$$

Question 13.16.

For our 45-strike put that we've written: $P_1 = 5.3596$, $\Delta_1 = -.6051$, $\Gamma_1 = .0457$. The 40-strike has $C_2 = 4.1217$, $\Delta_2 = .6151$, $\Gamma_2 = .0454$. Since we are "short" gamma (we wrote an option), we must buy $\Gamma_1 / \Gamma_2 = .0457/.0454 = 1.007$ 40-strike calls. Our option position will have a total delta of $.6051 + (1.007) \, .6151 = 1.2245$ hence we have to short 1.2247 shares. Our total initial cash flow will be $5.3596 - 1.007 \, (4.1217) + 1.2247 \, (40) = 50.20$. Using primes to denote next day prices, our one-day profit will be

$$-P_1' - 1.007 C_2' - 1.2247 S' + 50.20 e^{.08/365} \tag{8}$$

We use Black Scholes with $T - t = 179/365$ to arrive at our profit in Figure 8.

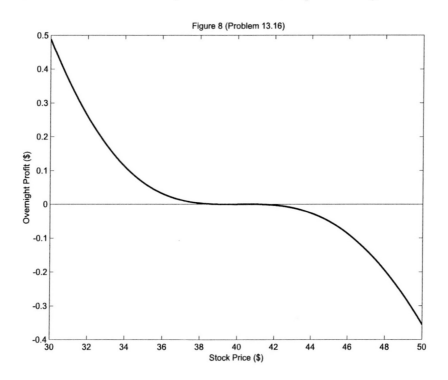

Figure 8 (Problem 13.16)

Question 13.18.

The relevant values of the spread are: $f = 5.0824 - 2(1.9905) = 1.1014$, $\Delta = -.71845 - 2(-.4176) = .11675$, and $\Gamma = .05633 - 2(.06516) = -.07399$. Since we wrote the spread, to Γ hedge we need to buy $.07399/.04536 = 1.6312$ options. The delta of the spread and the call will become $.11675 + (1.6312)(.6151) = 1.120$; therefore we need to short 1.120 shares. The graph of our profit is given in Figure 10.

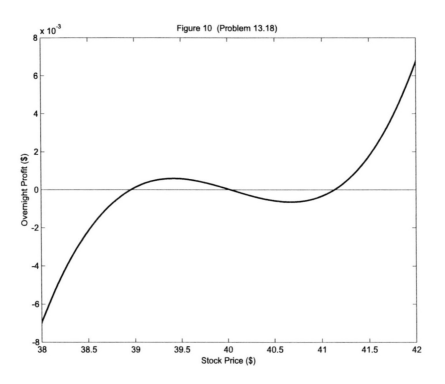

Question 13.20.

We purchased a 91-day 40-strike call, denoted option 1.

a)   Using a 180-day 40-strike call (option 2) to delta-rho hedge we must write 50.64 of these options and short 27.09 shares of stock. Our one day profit is given in Figure 13.

b)   Using option 2 as well as a one year (365 day) 45-strike put (option 3) to delta-gamma-vega hedge, we have the following solution: $n_2 = -1.2259$, $n_3 = -.2874$, and $n_S = .0307$. The one day profit is given in Figure 14 on the next page. If we added another option, call it option 4, we can try to hedge all of the greeks (note Θ will be taken care of by the Black Scholes Equation). Let Vega be noted by v

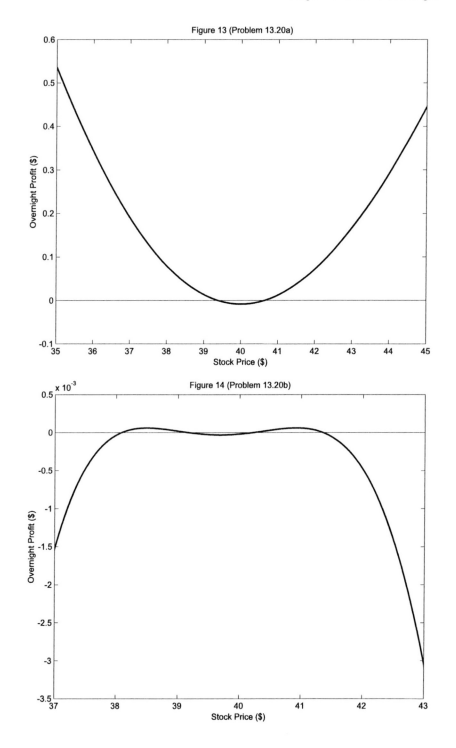

$$\Delta_2 n_2 + \Delta_3 n_3 + \Delta_4 n_4 + n_S = -.5824 \tag{9}$$

$$\Gamma_2 n_2 + \Gamma_3 n_3 + \Gamma_4 n_4 = -.0652 \tag{10}$$

$$v_2 n_2 + v_3 n_3 + v_4 n_4 = -.0780 \tag{11}$$

$$\text{Rho}_2 n_2 + \text{Rho}_3 n_3 + \text{Rho}_4 n_4 = -.0511 \tag{12}$$

These are four equations and four unknowns (the coefficients are from the Black Scholes model). Note we must try to solve the last three equations simultaneously, which give us the position of the three options, and then use the underlying asset to delta hedge.

On a related note, occasionally you will find strange things may happen when we use options with the same maturity. For a given time to maturity, vega and gamma are proportional (i.e. $v_i = k_i \Gamma_i$). If two options have the same time to maturity, then $k_1 = k_2$. If we use option 2 to gamma hedge a position of option 1, $\Gamma_2 n_2 = -n_1 \Gamma_1$; with the same maturity, we have

$$v_2 n_2 = k_2 \Gamma_2 n_2 = -k_1 n_1 \Gamma_1 = -n_1 v_1. \tag{13}$$

Hence gamma hedging takes care of vega hedging if the maturity matches. Similarly, if we use two options (call the 2 and 3) of the same maturity to hedge an option (call it 1) position with a different maturity we will have a problem for $\Gamma_2 n_2 + \Gamma_3 n_3 = -n_1 \Gamma_1$ implies

$$v_2 n_2 + v_3 n_3 = k_2 (\Gamma_2 n_2 + \Gamma_3 n_3) = -k_2 n_1 \Gamma_1 = -\left(\frac{k_2}{k_1}\right) n_1 v_1. \tag{14}$$

If $k_1 \neq k_2$ (i.e. the option being hedged is different from the two traded options' identical time to maturity), it will be impossible to both gamma and vega hedge. A simple algebraic way of looking at this is by trying to solve

$$ax + by = c \tag{15}$$
$$2(ax + by) = kc \tag{16}$$

Unless $k = 2$ (in which case we have an infinite number of solutions), there will be no solution.

Chapter 14
Exotic Options: I

Question 14.2.

The arithmetic average is 5 (three 5's, one 4, and one 6) and the geometric average is $(5 \times 4 \times 5 \times 6 \times 5)^{1/5} = 4.9593$. For the next sequence, the arithmetic average does not change ($= 5$); however the geometric average, $(3 \times 4 \times 5 \times 6 \times 7)^{1/5} = 4.7894$ is much lower. As the standard deviation increases (holding arithmetic means constant), the geometric return decreases. As an example, suppose we have two observations, $1 + \sigma$ and $1 - \sigma$. The arithmetic mean will be 1; however the geometric mean will be $\sqrt{(1 + \sigma)(1 - \sigma)} = \sqrt{1 - \sigma^2} < 1$.

Question 14.4.

Using the forward tree specification, $u = \exp(.08/2 + .3/\sqrt{2}) = 1.2868, d = \exp(.08/2 - .3/\sqrt{2})$ $= .84187$, and risk neutral probability $p = (e^{.08/2} - d)/(u - d) = .44716$. The two possible prices in 6 months are 128.68 and 84.19; the three possible 1 year prices are 165.58, 108.33, and 70.87. Using the 6m and 12m prices, the possible arithmetic averages are (in 1 year) are 147.13, 118.50, 96.26, and 77.53. The four possible geometric averages are 145.97, 118.07, 95.50, and 77.24. These are in the order: u-u, u-d, d-u, and d-d.

a)   The four intrinsic values will be $165.58 - 147.13 = 18.45$ (u-u), 0 (u-d), $108.33 - 96.26 = 12.07$ (d-u), and zero (d-d). This will give an up value of $e^{-.04}p18.45 = 7.93$, a down value of $e^{-.04}p12.07 = 5.19$, and an initial value of $e^{-.04}(p7.93 + (1 - p)5.19) = 6.1602$.

b)   The four intrinsic values will be $165.58 - 145.97 = 19.61$ (u-u), zero (u-d), $108.33 - 95.50 = 12.83$ (d-u), and zero (d-d). This will give an up value of $e^{-.04}p19.61 = 8.43$ and a down value of $e^{-.04}p12.83 = 5.51$ with an initial value of $e^{-.04}(p8.43 + (1 - p)5.51) = 6.55$.

Question 14.6.

a)   A standard call is worth 4.1293.

b)   A knock in call will also be worth 4.1293 (you can verify this with the software). In order for the standard call to ever be in the money, it must pass through the barrier. They therefore give identical payoffs.

c)   Similar reasoning, implies the knock-out will be worthless since in order for $S_T > 45$, the barrier must have been hit making knocking out the option.

Question 14.8.

See Table Three for the prices and ratio. The longer the time to expiration, the greater the dispersion of S_T. For the standard put option, this increases the value unless the option expiration starts to become large (we lose time value of receiving the strike price). For the knock-out, there is an extra negative effect a higher expiration date has. With higher dispersion of S_T, the greater chance for larger S_T, the greater the chance of being knocked out; however, there will also be a higher chance for the barrier to be hit.

Table Three (Problem 14.8)

T	Standard	Knock-Out	Ratio
0.25	5.0833	3.8661	1.3148
0.5	5.3659	3.4062	1.5753
1	5.6696	2.8626	1.9806
2	5.7862	2.2233	2.6025
3	5.6347	1.8109	3.1115
4	5.3736	1.5094	3.5601
5	5.0654	1.2761	3.9695
100	0.0012	0.0001	24.4951

Question 14.10.

When $K = 0.9$, the only scenarios where the up and out puts have a different payoff than the standard put is where the exchange rate rises to the barrier of 1 (or 1.05) before six months (i.e. $x_t > 1$ for $t < T$) and then end below .9 (i.e. $x_T < .9$). In this case, the up and out puts will pay nothing (they will have gotten knocked out) and the standard put will pay the intrinsic value $.9 - x_T$. Given the volatility assumption, these scenarios are virtually impossible and, for the small chance that they happen, the payoff in for the standard put would be small.

When $K = 1$ the scenarios mentioned above are much more likely as x only has to rise above 1 (or 1.05) and then finish below 1. With higher time to expirations, the probabilities of such scenarios will become non negligible and we should expect the up and out to have lower values than the standards (when $K = .9$).

Question 14.12.

a)   3.6956

b)   In one year, the put option will be worth more than $2 if $S_1 < 44.35$.

c)   2.2978

d)   If we buy the standard put from part a) as well as this compound option for x we will keep the standard put if $S_1 < 44.35$ and sell it for $2 otherwise. This identical to putting $2e^{-.08}$ in the risk free bond and buying the compound option in part c). The total costs must be identical implying $3.6956 + x = 2.2978 + 2e^{-.08}$, implying $x = .448$.

Question 14.14.

Using $\sigma = 30\%$, $r = 8\%$, and $\delta = 0$. See Figure Two on the next page. When we are close to maturity (e.g. $T = 1/52$) we see large variations in delta. The discontinuity at K_2 can require deltas greater than one. The value of the option can go from close to zero to close to $10 with little movement in the price (if S_T is close to K_1). If $T \simeq 0$, delta will be close zero for $S < 100$, enormous for $S = 100$, and close to one if $S > 100$. This problem does not occur as T becomes larger.

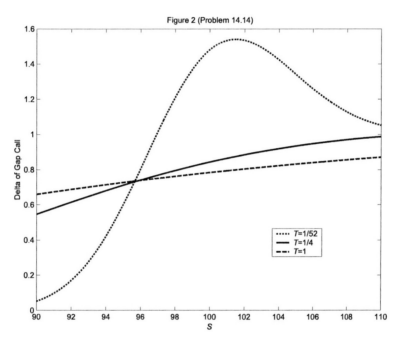

Figure 2 (Problem 14.14)

Question 14.16.

Under Black Scholes the standard 40-strike call on S will be

$$BSCall(40, 40, .3, .08, 1, 0).\tag{1}$$

For the exchange option on S using $2/3$ of a share of Q as the strike, we use a strike of $(2/3)\,60 = 40$, a volatility of $\sqrt{.3^2 + .5^2 - 2(.5)(.3)(.5)} = .43589$, and an "interest rate" of .04:

$$BSCall(40, 40, .43589, .04, T, 0).\tag{2}$$

For, all but very long time to maturities, the higher volatility will offset the lower "interest" and the exchange option will be worth more. With $T = 1$, we have the standard option is worth 6.28 and the exchange option is worth 7.58.

Question 14.18.

a) $Var\,[\ln(S/Q)] = .3^2 + .3^2 - 2\,(.3)\,(.3) = 0$ and the option is worthless (it will never be in the money as $S_T = Q_T$).

b) $Var\,[\ln(S/Q)] = .3^2 + .4^2 - 2\,(.3)\,(.4) = .01$ hence we use a 10% volatility in Black-Scholes. With $T = 1$ we have the exchange option equal to \$1.60.

c)   If $\ln(S)$ and $\ln(Q)$ are jointly normal with $\rho = 1$ then they are linearly related. Hence

$$\ln(Q) = \ln(40)\left(1 - \frac{\sigma_Q}{\sigma_S}\right) + \frac{\sigma_Q}{\sigma_S}\ln(S)\,. \tag{3}$$

In question a), $\ln(Q) = \ln(S) \implies Q = S$. For question b),

$$\ln(Q) = -\frac{\ln(40)}{3} + \frac{4}{3}\ln(S) \implies Q = .2924S^{4/3}\,. \tag{4}$$

If S rises (say $S_T = 50$) then Q will be greater than S (say $Q_T = 53.861$); the option will be in the money if S falls for Q will fall by a greater amount making the exchange option have value.

Question 14.20.

a)   Since the options will be expiring at t_1, we have the payoff of a put if $S_T < K$ and the payoff of a call if $S_T > K$. This is equivalent to a K strike straddle.

b)   Using put-call parity at t_1, the value of the as-you-like-it option at t_1 will be:

$$\max\left(C\,(S_1, K, T - t_1), C\,(S_1, K, T - t_1) + Ke^{-r(T-t_1)} - Se^{-\delta(T-t_1)}\right) \tag{5}$$

$$= C\,(S_1, K, T - t_1) + \max\left(0, Ke^{-r(T-t_1)} - Se^{-\delta(T-t_1)}\right) \tag{6}$$

$$= C\,(S_1, K, T - t_1) + e^{-\delta(T-t_1)}\max\left(0, Ke^{(\delta-r)(T-t_1)} - S\right)\,. \tag{7}$$

The first term is the value of a call with strike K and maturity T; the second term is the payoff from holding $e^{-\delta(T-t_1)}$ put options that expire at t_1 with strike $Ke^{(\delta-r)(T-t_1)}$.

Question 14.22.

a)   \$6.0831

b)   The current price of a 1m 95-strike put is 1.2652. In fact, a 1m put with a strike equal to 95% of the stock price will always be equal to 1.2652% of the stock price. Therefore, the present value of twelve of these 1m 95% strike puts is $12\,(1.2652) = 15.182$.

c)   Technically, and perhaps non-intuitively, the rolling insurance strategy costs more because it is more expensive to replicate. Note that one strategy doesn't dominate another. If the price never falls less than 5% in month, all of the 12 one month options will be worthless; yet the price in 1 year could have fallen by more than 5%. Interest aside, the rollover options will give the holder $\sum_{i=0}^{11} \max(S_{i+1} - .95S_i, 0)$; whereas, the simple insurance gives the holder $\max(S_{12} - .95S_0, 0)$. The rollover strategy has the advantage of being able to provide payoffs (insurance) for each month regardless of the past. If the stock price rises in one month to (say) $120, the simple insurance option will be less effective whereas the rollover will provide a new insurance option with a strike of $.95(120) = 114$.

Chapter 15
Financial Engineering and Security Design

Question 15.2.

For this problem let $B = \frac{1}{1.03}$.

a)   The prepaid forward price is $1200e^{-.015(3)} = 1147.20$.

b)   We have to solve the coupon, c, that solves

$$c\left(\sum_{i=1}^{6} B^i\right) + 1147.20 = 1200 \Longrightarrow c = 52.8\left(\frac{1-B}{B-B^7}\right) = 9.7467. \tag{1}$$

c)   The prepaid forward price for 1 share at time t is $F_t^P = 1200e^{-.015t}$; for each semi-annual share, we can write the relevant prepaid forward price as $1200D^i$ where $D = e^{-.015/2}$. With this formulation we have a similar analysis for the fractional shares, c^*:

$$c^*\left(\sum_{i=1}^{6} D^i\right)1200 + 1147.20 = 1200 \Longrightarrow c^* = \frac{52.8}{1200}\left(\frac{1-D}{D-D^7}\right) = .007528 \text{ shares.} \tag{2}$$

Note this is interpreted as we will receive .007528 units of the index every six months. This has a current value of $1200\,(.007528) = 9.0336$. We could quote c^* in dollars (9.0336) instead of units.

Question 15.4.

The relevant 2 year interest rate is $\ln(1/.8763)/2 = 6.6\%$.

a)   The embedded option is worth 247.88. The prepaid forward is worth $1200e^{-.015(2)} = 1164.53$. The bond price is worth the sum $1164.53 + 247.88 = 1412.41$.

b) λ must solve $1164.53 + \lambda247.88 = 1200 \Longrightarrow \lambda = 35.47/247.88 = .1431$.

Question 15.6.

We continue to use 6.6% as the relevant 2 year interest rate.

a)   The out of the money option (i.e. $K = 1500$) is worth 141.54, making the bond have a value of $1164.53 + 247.88 - 141.54 = 1270.9$.

b)   We must solve $1164.53 + \lambda(247.88 - 141.54) = 1200$ for a solution of $\lambda = .3336$.

c)   If $\lambda = 1$, we have to adjust the strike (from part a, we know we have to lower K) to make the out of the option worth $C(K) = 1164.53 + 247.88 - 1200 = 212.41 \implies K \approx 1284$.

Question 15.8.

Using a semi-annual coupon of c, if the value of the CD is 1300, c and γ must solve

$$1300 = 1300e^{-.06\times5.5} + c\left(\sum_{i=1}^{11} e^{-.03i}\right) + \gamma 441.44. \tag{3}$$

This implies the participation rate, as a function of c is $\gamma = .82774 - .0209c$; i.e. a line with intercept .82774 and slope $-.0209$. For example, a \$10 semi annual coupon will require .618 74 call options to have the CD be worth 1300. If the bank would like to earn 5%, c and γ must solve

$$1300(1 - .05) = 1300e^{-.06\times5.5} + c\left(\sum_{i=1}^{11} e^{-.03i}\right) + \gamma 441.44. \tag{4}$$

This implies $\gamma = .6805 - .0209c$; this is a parallel line (to the previous answer's line) with a lower intercept.

Question 15.10.

The 2600-strike call has a value of 162.48. The 1300-strike put is worth 178.99. This implies λ must solve

$$1300 = 1300e^{-.06\times5.5} - 178.99 + \lambda(162.48) \tag{5}$$

implying $\lambda = 3.3505$.

Question 15.12.

See Table One for the numerical solution.

a)   The value is $1300e^{-r\times5.5} + .7 \times BSCall(1300, 1300, \sigma, r, 5.5, \delta)$.

Table One (Problem 15.12)

		0.06	0.06	0.06	0.05	0.07	0.06	0.06
	r	0.06	0.06	0.06	0.05	0.07	0.06	0.06
	σ	0.3	0.2	0.4	0.3	0.3	0.3	0.3
	δ	0.015	0.015	0.015	0.015	0.015	0.005	0.025
15.12a	V	1243.61	1183.16	1304.37	1278.54	1211.64	1280.15	1210.12
15.12b	γ	0.7000	0.8702	0.5850	0.6160	0.7684	0.6260	0.7851

b)   We must solve for γ,

$$1300\,(1 - .043) = 1300e^{-r \times 5.5} + \gamma \times BSCall\,(1300, 1300, \sigma, r, 5.5, \delta) \tag{6}$$

Question 15.14.

The two year, prepaid forward price is 17.351.

a) c^* must solve

$$c^* 20.5\,(.9388) + c^* 19.8\,(.8763) + 19.8\,(.8763) = 20.9 \tag{7}$$

Hence $c^* = \frac{20.9 - 17.351}{19.245 + 17.351} = .097$ barrels. In dollars, this is currently worth $.097\,(20.9) = \$2.0273$.

b)   Similarly,

$$c^* \left(\sum_{i=1}^{8} F_{t_i}^P \right) = 20.9 - 17.351 \tag{8}$$

hence $c^* = \frac{20.9 - 17.351}{152.1556} = .023325$ barrels, currently worth $.0233\,(20.9) = \$0.4875$.

Question 15.16.

For the options, we can use the following answer from part a) as the underlying in the non-dividend $BSCall$, the interest rate being $\ln\,(1/.9388) = 6.32\%$.

a)   The prepaid forward price is $F_i P_i = 20.5\,(.9388) = 19.2454$.

b)   With $K_1 = 19.577$ and $K_2 = 21.577$, a put with K_1 strike is worth .7436 and a call with strike K_2 is worth the same. Hence the cost is the same as the prepaid forward contract, 19.2454. With this contract, we receive the spot price of oil if S_1 is between 19.577 and 21.577. We receive a lower bound of 19.577 (if $S_1 < 19.577$) and an upper bound of 21.577 (if $S_1 > 21.577$). This payoff is similar to a bull spread with a risk free bond. The prepaid forward has the holder owning a barrel of oil; whereas, this contract, involves owning a barrel of oil only if S_1 is between K_1 and K_2. It will do worse than the prepaid forward if $S_1 > K_2$ and better if $S_1 < K_1$ (trading off upside to protect downside).

c)   The value of this claim is zero: $S_1 - 20.50$ is a (zero cost) forward contract and the two options have equal premiums. If S_1 is between K_1 and K_2, we pay 20.5 and receive a barrel of oil worth S_1. If $S_1 < K_1 = 19.577$, we pay 20.5, receive a barrel of oil, and sell it for K_1 leading to a cash flow of $19.577 - 20.5 = -.923$. If $S_1 > K_2 = 21.577$, we pay 20.5, receive a barrel of oil, and sell it for K_2 leading to a cash flow of $21.577 - 20.5 = 1.077$. This is the profit from a bull spread.

Question 15.18.

Since the contract has zero value, it doesn't matter which side of the contract we examine. Consider the "seller" of the contract. Each quarter i, the seller receives a cash flow

$$19.90 - \overline{F} + \max{(S_i - 19.90, 0)} - \max{(S_i - 21.90, 0)} \tag{9}$$

To check, if $S_i < 19.90$ the seller has a cash flow $19.90 - \overline{F}$, if S_i is between 19.90 and 21.90 there is a cash flow of $S_i - \overline{F}$, and if $S_i > 21.90$ the cash flow if $21.90 - \overline{F}$. Each quarter the bull spread will have a value

$$V_i = BSCall\,(F_i P_i, 19.90, .15, r_i, t_i, 0) - BSCall\,(F_i P_i, 21.90, .15, r_i, t_i, 0) \tag{10}$$

where P_i is zero coupon bond price from Problems Table and $e^{r_i t_i} = P_i$. Table Two shows the values for V_i and r_i. We now must solve for $\overline{F}$ in

$$V_{contract} = 0 = \sum_{i=1}^{8} (19.90 - \overline{F})\, P_i + \sum_{i=1}^{8} V_i \tag{11}$$

implying

$$\overline{F} = \frac{\sum_{i=1}^{8} V_i}{\sum_{i=1}^{8} P_i} + 19.90 = \frac{6.3616}{7.4475} + 19.90 = 20.754. \tag{12}$$

Table Two (Problem 15.18)

Quarter	1	2	3	4	5	6	7	8
F	21	21.1	20.8	20.5	20.2	20	19.9	19.8
P	0.9852	0.9701	0.9546	0.9388	0.9231	0.9075	0.8919	0.8763
F*P	20.6892	20.46911	19.85568	19.2454	18.64662	18.15	17.74881	17.35074
r	0.059642	0.060712	0.06195	0.063153	0.064014	0.064708	0.065372	0.066023
V of Spread	1.00798	1.00023	0.880993	0.791487	0.718889	0.675769	0.653802	0.632465

Question 15.20.

The main textbook gives the following table of payment at maturity of the Times Mirror PEPS:

Underlying price of Netscape at expiration			Payoff to DECS holder
	S(T)	<$39.25	S(T)
$39.25 <	S(T)	< $45.14	$39.25
$45.14 <	S(T)		$39.25 + 0.8696 * (S(T) − $45.14)

The above table can be replicated with the following instruments: buy one share of Netscape, sell one Netscape call with a strike of $39.25, and buy 0.8696 calls with a strike of $45.14.

Furthermore, we need to take care of the dividends of the PEPS. We are entitled to the annual cash dividend of $1.67 (which is the issue price of $39.25 times the coupon rate of 4.25%) of the PEPS (which is missing from the above strategy). We therefore need to add zero-coupon bonds characterizing the PEPS dividend payments.

$$P_{PEPS} = S_T - C(39.25, \ldots) + 0.8696 \times C(45.14) + PV(Div_{PEPS})$$

We can value the annual PEPS dividend

	R	0.07	
PEPS			
Div		1.668125	
		P(t)	disc. DECS Div
	1	0.932	1.555
	2	0.869	1.450
	3	0.811	1.352
	4	0.756	1.261
	5	0.705	1.176
			6.794

Therefore, we can solve: $P_{PEPS} = 39.25 - 16.302 + 0.8696 \times 18.153 + 6.794 = 42.067$.

The PEPS is worth $42.067 today.

Question 15.22.

a)   We have to value a forward contract with a dividend yield of zero. We know that the price for such a forward contract is:

$$F_{0,T} = S_0 \times \exp(rt) = 100 \times \exp(0.03 \times 3) = 109.417$$

b)	We could see in part a) that the forward price is taking into account the interest accruing to the $100. The annual payment, if the price agreed upon is $100, would reflect that interest. The coupon would have to be 3%, continuously compounded, or $3.045, at the end of year 1, 2, and 3.

c)	Now, we can depict the payoff of the stock purchase contract as follows:

Underlying stock price at expiration	Payoff to stock purchase contract holder
$S(T) < \$100.00$	$1 * S(T)$
$\$100 \le S(T) < \$116.20$	$S(T) + (\$100 - S(T)) = \$100$
$\dfrac{\$100}{\$116.20} \le S(T)$	$S(T) + (\$100 - S(T)) + 100/116.20 * (S(T) - \$116.20)$

Therefore, we can value this complicated stock purchase contract as a simple stock purchase contract for a price of $100 plus the simultaneous purchase of 100/116.20 call options with a strike of 116.20 and a sale of one call option with a strike of $100. We valued the simple stock purchase contract in part b), and now have to value the two stock options:

Based on the information given in the exercise, we obtain:

$$C(100) = 24.2068$$
$$C(116.20) = 18.1729$$

Overall, we have:

$$Payoff = S_T - 100 + \max(0, S_T - 100) + \frac{100}{116.20} \times \max(0, S_T - 116.20)$$

and a price today of:

$$\begin{aligned} Price &= -\sum_{t=1}^{3} \$3.045 \times \exp(-0.03 \times t) + 24.2068 - 0.8606 \times 18.1729 \\ &= -8.6056 + 24.2068 - 15.6396 \\ &= -\$0.0384 \end{aligned}$$

We would need to be paid 3.84 cents to enter into the contract.

d)	Now, we are not entitled to receive the dividend the stock pays. This is an inconvenience, and we have to take this into account when calculating the forward price:

$$F_{0,T} = S_0 \times \exp((r - \delta) \times t) = 100 \times \exp((0.03 - 0.03) \times 3) = 100.00$$

$100 is now the fair price, and we would not have to pay a coupon in part b). For part c), we would pay up to $24.2068 - 15.6396 = 8.5672$ to enter the stock purchase contract with the contractual features described.

Chapter 16
Corporate Applications

Question 16.2.

Let K be the maturity value of the debt. Equity is valued as a call option with strike K on the assets $A = 100$, with the given interest and volatility. By Black Scholes, the four values of equity will be $E = 5.9977, 11.4278, 23.3041$, and 37.0374; debt will be $D = 100 - E = 94.0023, 88.5722, 76.6959$, and 62.9626. Yields are given by $De^{yT} = K$ which implies $y = \ln(K/D)/T = 0.3042, 0.2118, 0.1495$, and 0.1245. The debt to equity ratios are $D/E = 15.6732, 7.7506, 3.2911$, and 1.7000.

Question 16.4.

The value and delta of the relevant 5 year call option is $E = 34.6653$ and $\Delta = .7453$. Using equation (16.7), the expected return on equity is

$$r_E = .08 + (.12 - .08)\frac{100\,(.7453)}{34.6653} = 16.60\%. \tag{1}$$

The volatility of equity is given by

$$\sigma_E E = \Delta \sigma_A A \Longrightarrow \sigma_E = \frac{\Delta \sigma_A A}{E} = \frac{100\,(.3)\,(.7453)}{34.6653} = 64.50\%. \tag{2}$$

Alternatively, since

$$r_E = r + \frac{(r_A - r)}{\sigma_A}\sigma_E \tag{3}$$

we can solve

$$\sigma_E = \sigma_A \frac{r_E - r}{r_A - r} = .3\frac{.086}{.04} = 64.5\%. \tag{4}$$

See Figures One, Two, and Three for the effect on expected returns when we vary A, σ, and r. For changes in r we assume that r_A changes by the same amount (i.e. the risk premium on assets is constant at $r_A - r = 4\%$).

Question 16.6.

a) $y = \ln(100/D)/5 = 0.1585, 0.0853, 0.0678, 0.0627$, and 0.0600.

b)   See Table Three.

116

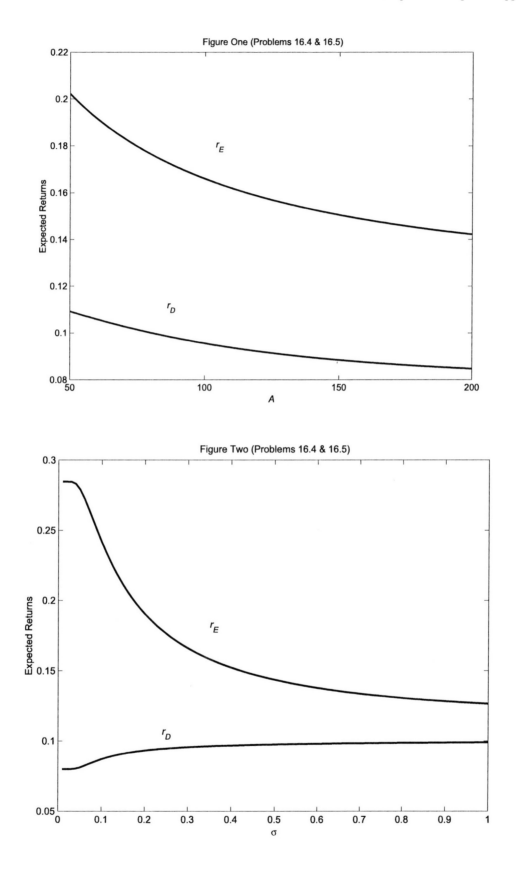

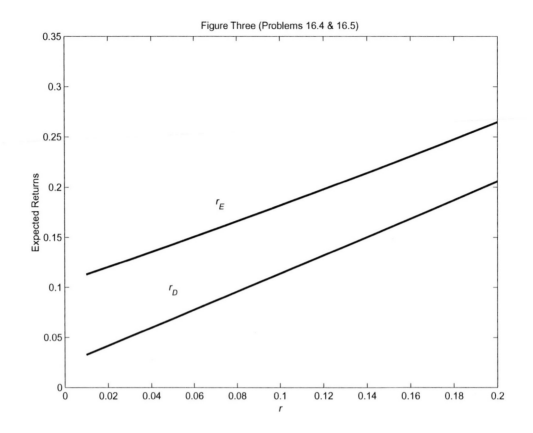

Figure Three (Problems 16.4 & 16.5)

Table Three (Problem 16.6b)

Volatility	Yield on Debt
0.10	0.0653
0.15	0.0732
0.20	0.0825
0.25	0.0926
0.30	0.1034
0.35	0.1148
0.40	0.1266
0.45	0.1390
0.50	0.1519
0.55	0.1652
0.60	0.1791
0.65	0.1934
0.70	0.2082
0.75	0.2236
0.80	0.2394
0.85	0.2557
0.90	0.2725
0.95	0.2898
1.00	0.3077

Question 16.8.

Let V be the market value of the new project and let k be the cost of the project ($V - k$ would be the NPV). If the project is paid for with junior debt of face value F, then the junior debt must be worth k; this implies

$$\text{Junior Debt Value} = C(100 + V, 150) - C(100 + V, 150 + F) = k. \tag{5}$$

Shareholders wealth, if they do the project, will be $C(100 + V, 150 + F)$. Hence the change in their wealth is

$$C(100 + V, 150 + F) - C(100, 150) = C(100 + V, 150) - C(100, 150) - k. \tag{6}$$

$C(100, 150) = 26.0672$ is the initial value of shareholders wealth. When $k = 1$, shareholders' wealth would rise if $C(100 + V, 150) > 26.0672 + 1 \Longrightarrow V > 1.5806$. When $k = 10$, shareholders wealth would rise if $V > 14.9817$. When $k = 25$, shareholders wealth would rise if $V > 35.1288$. These are solved numerically; you can use Δ (and Γ) to approximate them algebraically.

Question 16.10.

Using equation (16.12):

a) $(20/22)\text{BSCall}(5, 15, .3, .08, 5, 0) = .3209$ per share which is .6418 in total.

b) $(20/35)\text{BSCall}(5, 20, .3, .08, 10, 0) = .5601$ per share which is $15(.5601) = 8.4015$ in total.

Question 16.12.

The debt is worth $D = A - BSCall(100, 200, .30, .08, 10, 0) = 60.1035$. The warrants are worth $\frac{20}{28}BSCall\left(\frac{100}{20}, 25, .30, .08, 10, 0\right) = .5191$ per share which is $8(.5191) = 4.1528$ in total. Equity is the residual, $E = 100 - 60.1035 - 4.1528 = 35.744$ or $35.744/20 = 1.7872$ per share.

Question 16.14.

A risk free bond would be $100e^{-.06(5)} = 74.082$. The 3 call options would be worth $3BSCall(22.278, 33.333, .30, .06, 5, 0) = 15.094$ for a total of $74.082 + 15.094 = 89.176$. This is (slightly) underestimates the value due to default risk.

Question 16.16.

The expected number of years to exercise is computed as $1(.1) + 2(.1) + 3(.8) = 2.7$. If we use 2.7 years as the time to expiration in the Black-Scholes formula, we get a price of

BSCall(100, 100, .3, .08, 2.7, 0) = 28.91. The Black-Scholes premiums for one, two, and three years to expiration are 15.71 (1 year), 24.02 (2 years), and 30.85 (3 years). The expected value of the options is

$$.1\,(15.71) + .1\,(24.02) + .8\,(30.85) = 28.65. \tag{7}$$

The answer is different depending upon whether we use the average time to maturity to compute an option price, or whether we compute the average option price. The second procedure—averaging the option values with different times to maturity—is correct. To see this, imagine that we have a large number of executives with options, who have identical probabilities of survival and option grants. If the group were large enough, we could be sure that 10% of the executives would die each of the first two years, and 80% would exercise after 3 years. Since the company has given options to the executives, it has a short position in call options. The company could hedge its obligation to this group of executives by buying 10% 1 year options, 10% 2-year options, and 80% 3-year options. This yields an option cost per executive of 28.65. The 2.7-year option, by contrast, is a fiction which does not correspond to anything real.

Question 16.18.

These are forward start options. Each option has time to maturity of 5 years. Since there are no dividends, receiving a 5 year ATM option in t years is equivalent to receiving a 5 year ATM option today. Hence we can add them up (they all have the same value),

$$Value = 30000BSCall\,(100, 100, .30, .08, 5, 0) = \$1,260,340. \tag{8}$$

Question 16.20.

a)   This makes the amount paid (as a function of S_A) continuous at the collar points; i.e. $1.714\,(35) = 60$ and $1.333\,(45) = 60$; i.e. $1.714 = 60/35$ and $1.333 = 60/45$.

b)   The deal can be looked at as giving Company B's shareholders 1.333 shares of A, a short position on 1.714 of 35-strike puts, and a long position of 1.333 of 45-strike puts. If $S_A > 45$, both options are out of the money and we have 1.333 shares of A. If $35 \leq S_A \leq 45$ we sell our 1.333 shares for $45. If $S_A \leq 35$ we sell our 1.333 shares for 45 but have to buy 1.714 shares for 35. By design, see the previous answer, these amounts are the same (we receive 60 and pay 60). We are now left with 1.714 shares of company B. The value of this offer is

$$\frac{4}{3}\,(S_A + P\,(45)) - \frac{60}{35}P\,(35) = \frac{4}{3}\,(47.3422) - \frac{60}{35}2.4283 = 58.96. \tag{9}$$

c)   For volatilities ranging from 20% to over 60%, the value stays between 58.65 and 59.

Question 16.22.

We can value the options using the Black-Scholes spreadsheet and the inputs given in the text. We have:

$$Call(44.50, 44.50, 0.566, 0.06, 4.9, 0) = 24.31243$$
$$Call(63.25, 63.25, 0.566, 0.06, 4.9, 0) = 34.55642$$
$$Call(63.25, 44.50, 0.566, 0.06, 4.9, 0) = 40.11634$$

Note that for the Black-Scholes formula we have: $63.25/44.50 * Call(44.50, 44.50) = Call(63.25, 63.25)$.

Ms. Tagliaferro does not seem to understand option pricing. From the above results, it is evident that the stock price around the grant matters very much for the cost to the company. Most likely, Ms. Tagliaferro confuses intrinsic value and true option price. It is true that the intrinsic value to the employee is zero before the options vest, because he cannot get the money.

However, the company should be concerned with its cost, which is measured by the Black-Scholes price.

If the board knew about the earnings surprise when they granted the option package (which is very likely), they wasted a lot of their shareholders' money. Their decision to give the CEO a 44.50 at-the-money option grant when they knew the stock price would rise to 63.25 cost shareholders $[C(63.25, 44.50) - C(63.25, 63.25)] * 600,000 = \$3,335,952$.

Question 16.24.

The following spreadsheet contains the answer:

Inputs					
Stock price	100			h	1
Strike Price	100			u	1.3499
Volatility	30%			d	0.7408
Domestic r	0.05			exp(r*h)	1.0513
Dividend	0			exp(divyld*h)	1
Time to Maturity	3			Prob up	0.5097
0=Forward tree;					
1=CRR	1			Prob Down	0.4903

Stock price process:

100.00	134.99	182.21	245.96
	74.08	100.00	134.99
		54.88	74.08
			40.66

Intrinsic value

0.00	34.99	82.21	145.96
	0.00	0.00	34.99
		0.00	0.00
			0.00

One-period value

16.96	39.86	87.09	0.00
	0.00	16.96	0.00
		0.00	0.00
			0.00

Two-period value

19.33	50.14	87.09
	8.23	16.96
		0.00

Reported Expense

19.33	10.28	0.00
	8.23	0.00
		0.00

PV(expense)

28.1473078	10.2759199	0.00
	8.22549925	0.00
		0.00

The present value of the option deductions is 28.147, as was to be shown. Remember that you have to compare the two-period value of 50.14 against the one-period value of 39.86.

Chapter 17
Real Options

Question 17.2.

If invest at time T you receive the (at time T) an "NPV"

$$NPV_T = \frac{.8\,(1.02)^{T+1}}{1.05} + \frac{.8\,(1.02)^{T+2}}{1.05^2} - 1.5 \tag{1}$$

$$= (1.02)^T\, X - 1.5 \tag{2}$$

where $X = .8\,(1.02/1.05) + .8\,(1.02/1.05)^2$. This is growing at a decreasing rate; we can show this by looking at the growth rate

$$g_t = \frac{NPV_{t+1} - NPV_t}{NPV_t} = \frac{.02}{1 - \left(\frac{1.5}{X(1.02)^t}\right)}. \tag{3}$$

Notice $g_0 = .02/\,(1 - 1.5/X) = .955$ and as t gets very large g_t approaches .02. The key insight is that if we invest in the machine, you will be receiving the NPV and this cash grows at 5% (the risk free rate). Therefore, it is not optimal for you to invest if the NPV is growing at a higher rate; i.e. if $g_t > 5\%$ then you should not invest. If $g_t < 5\%$, you should have invested. Therefore we need to solve $g_T = 5\%$ for the optimal time T to invest:

$$\frac{.02}{1 - \left(\frac{1.5}{X(1.02)^T}\right)} = .05 \implies T = 24.727 \text{ years.} \tag{4}$$

The NPV (today's NPV) is

$$\frac{X\,(1.02)^{24.727} - 1.5}{1.05^{24.727}} = .29926. \tag{5}$$

The harder way to do this problem is to maximize the log of the NPV directly.

$$\ln(NPV) = \ln\left(\frac{X\,(1.02)^T - 1.5}{1.05^T}\right), \tag{6}$$

which is a calculus exercise (set the derivative equal to zero). The answer ($NPV = .29931$ and $T = 25.224$) will be slightly off due to using simple interest rates.

Question 17.4.

See Table One on the next page.

Table One (Problem 17.4)

Year (t)	Widget Price	NPV at t	NPV of Policy
0		27.00	27.00
1	0.55	29.20	27.81
2	0.57	31.49	28.56
3	0.59	33.87	29.26
4	0.62	36.34	29.90
5	0.64	38.92	30.49
6	0.67	41.59	31.04
7	0.70	44.38	31.54
8	0.72	47.27	32.00
9	0.75	50.28	32.41
10	0.78	53.41	32.79
11	0.81	56.67	33.13
12	0.85	60.06	33.44
13	0.88	63.58	33.72
14	0.92	67.24	33.96
15	0.95	71.05	34.18
16	0.99	75.01	34.36
17	1.03	79.13	34.53
18	1.07	83.42	34.66
19	1.11	87.88	34.78
20	1.16	92.51	34.87
21	1.21	97.33	34.94
22	1.25	102.35	34.99
23	1.30	107.56	35.02
24	**1.36**	**112.98**	**35.03**
25	**1.41**	**118.62**	**35.03**
26	1.47	124.49	35.01
27	1.52	130.59	34.98
28	1.59	136.93	34.93
29	1.65	143.53	34.87
30	1.72	150.39	34.80
31	1.78	157.52	34.71
32	1.86	164.94	34.62
33	1.93	172.66	34.51
34	2.01	180.69	34.39
35	2.09	189.03	34.27
36	2.17	197.72	34.14
37	2.26	206.74	34.00
38	2.35	216.13	33.85
39	2.44	225.90	33.69
40	2.54	236.06	33.53
41	2.64	246.62	33.36
42	2.75	257.60	33.19
43	2.86	269.03	33.01
44	2.97	280.91	32.83
45	3.09	293.26	32.64
46	3.21	306.12	32.45
47	3.34	319.48	32.25
48	3.47	333.38	32.05
49	3.61	347.83	31.85
50	3.76	362.87	31.64
51	3.91		

Question 17.6.

a)   This can be looked at as a call option on the 1m shares with strike price $K = 50m$ with an infinite time to expiration (it pays no dividends). The price of the land should be worth $100m; the reason for this is the PV of the excavation cost $(PV(K))$ is zero for we should never exercise it early. Say the land was worth $75m. We could short 1 million shares (receive $100m), buy the land and put the $25m in the risk free asset. Eventually that $25m will grow to over $50m and the buried shares will be able to cover our short sale.

b)   By similar reasoning, let the land be worth C and suppose we do the same exercise except this time we cover our short sale by digging up the shares just before the dividend gets paid. In 10 years we will have a cash flow (in $ millions), $(100 - C)\, e^{.05(10)} - 50$. This must be equal to zero, i.e. the land is worth

$$C = 100 - 50e^{-.5} = 69.673. \tag{7}$$

c)   This can now be treated as a perpetual American call on the stock with dividend yield 1%; it will have a value of 75.26 and should get exercised at $S = 500$.

Question 17.8.

a)   Each period, the expected price of a widget is $.25/2 + 2.25/2 = \$1.25$.

b)   The expected cash flow each period is

$$\frac{.25 - 1}{2} + \frac{2.25 - 1}{2} = .25 \tag{8}$$

which will have an NPV of $.25/.05 - 10 = -5$. It will never be optimal to produce.

c)   If we can only produce when the widget price is 2.25 we can have expected cash flows of $1.25/2 = .625$ (i.e. the second term in the above equation). This will use an $NPV = .625/.05 - 10 = 2.5$. This NPV is the same hence we do not have to consider delaying the project.

d)   If the widget price is either $\$.10$ or $\$2.40$ with equal probability, then the expected widget price remains $1.25, but expected cash flow is $.50\,(0) + .50(\$2.50 - \$1) = \$.75$ which increases our NPV to 5. Note that if the variance of the widget price is greater, expected cash flow is greater. In effect, producing only when it is profitable amounts to having a call option each period, with the strike price being the marginal cost of production. Increases in volatility raise the value of this call.

Question 17.10.

a)   We have to calculate the discount rate using the CAPM.

We have: $\alpha = 0.06 - 0.50 \times (0.10 - 0.06) = 0.04$

The expected cash flow is:

$$E(X) = 0.6 \times 50 + 0.4 \times 100 = 70.$$

We can calculate V, which is the value of the project as

$$V = \frac{E(X)}{(1+\alpha)^T} = \frac{70}{(1+0.04)^1} = 67.3077.$$

b)   In order to calculate the risk-neutral probability, we need

$$F_{0,1} = 67.3077 \times 1.06 = 71.3462.$$

The risk-neutral probability is:

$$p^* = \frac{F_{0,T} - X_d}{X_u - X_d} = \frac{71.3462 - 100}{50 - 100} = 0.573.$$

Hence, we can use the formula to evaluate:

$$V = \frac{0.5731 \times 50 + (1 - 0.5731) \times 100}{1.06} = 67.307$$

Question 17.12.

The discount rate is $r + \beta (r_m - r) = .05 + .5 (.08) = .09$. The current value of the future cash flows will be $8/.09 = 88.889$. The static NPV is negative at $88.89 - 100 = -11.11$. Using the binomial model, we need a dividend yield. As in the widget problem, the dividend yield will be the cash flow divided by the PV of the cash flows which is just the discount rate .09. For our options analysis we must use $r = \ln (1.05)$ and $\delta = \ln (1.04)$. Using a 3-step forward tree, see Table Two, we see we would invest in the project in two years in the up-up node; this gives a value of 12.45. With over 100 steps the project has a value around 12.34. With perpetual investment rights we could use the perpetual call real option

$$\text{CallPerpetual} (8/.09, 100, .35, \ln (1.05), \ln (1.09)) = \{19.64, 199.28\}. \tag{9}$$

The project is worth 19.64; i.e. the right to invest after three years adds approx. 50% to the project value.

Table Two (Problem 17.12)

Time (yrs)	1	2	3
			227.0623
			127.0623
		166.1037	
		66.10367	
	121.510371		112.7558
	28.8305216		12.75582
PV(CF) 88.88889		82.48464	
V of Proj. 12.45509		5.021933	
	60.3402646		55.99288
	1.97712275		0
		40.96066	
		0	
			27.80524
American Call			0

Strike = 100
Vol = 35.00%; r = 4.88%
Exp = 3 years; Div = 8.62%
u = 1.367; d = 0.679
Risk-neutral prob of up = 0.413
Forward tree

Question 17.14.

The residual value of the land effectively lowers the extraction costs (i.e. the strike price) by $R = 1$. We must now solve as in the examples:

$$S_t = \frac{\ln(1.05)}{\ln(1.04)} 12.60 = 15.674. \tag{10}$$

It will take t years where $15(1.009615)^t = 15.674$ for a solution of $t = 4.5932$. The value of the land is the NPV which will be

$$\frac{15.674 - 12.60}{1.05^{4.5932}} = 2.4568. \tag{11}$$

This is higher than extracting now, which would give us 2.40. Note the NPV (as of today) for extracting in T years is

$$\frac{1}{1.05^T}\left(15\frac{1.05^T}{1.04^T} - 13.60 + 1\right) = \frac{15}{1.04^T} - \frac{12.60}{1.05^T} \tag{12}$$

and we could maximize this directly.

Question 17.16.

If shutdown and start-up were costless, we would only produce if $S > 8$ and we would shut down if $S < 8$; hence $S_* = S^* = 8$. If there is no cost of undoing options there will be no hysteresis (e.g. producers will never be producing at a loss).

Question 17.18.

As in Example 17.1, we receive an underlying cash flow worth $300/.03 = 10000$ by paying a strike of the mine cost plus the PV of the cost of extraction $250/.05 + 1000 = 6000$. Note the dividend implied by the lease rate is $10000\,(.03) = 300$ and equal to the interest cost on the strike $6000\,(.05) = 300$. This implies there is no value to waiting. Using the call option method,

$$\text{CallPerpetual}\,(10000, 6000, .0001, \ln\,(1.05)\,, \ln\,(1.03)) = \{4000, 9903.68\}\,. \tag{13}$$

The mine is worth its current NPV.

Question 17.20.

The value of a producing mine is

$$V_p\,(S) = \frac{S}{.03} - 5000 + \text{PutPerpetual}\left(\frac{S}{.03}, \frac{250}{.05}, .2, \ln\,(1.05)\,, \ln\,(1.03)\right) \tag{14}$$

which is the value of not shutting down the mine plus the value of being able to shutdown. Working backwards, if $\overline{S}$ is the trigger price of our mine investment (i.e. we receive $V_p\,(\overline{S})$ when $S_t = \overline{S}$), the current value is

$$V\left(S, \overline{S}\right) = \left(\frac{300}{\overline{S}}\right)^{h_1} \times \left(V_p\,(\overline{S}) - 1000\right). \tag{15}$$

Using $h_1 = 1.5812$, we want to choose $\overline{S}$ to maximize the above quantity. Using Excel's solver or other numerical program $\overline{S} = 464.00$ and $V\,(300, \overline{S}) = 4830.21$. Note the trigger price is lower than when there is no shut down option.

Chapter 18
The Lognormal Distribution

Question 18.2.

If z is standard normal, $\mu + \sigma \times z$ is $\mathcal{N}(\mu, \sigma^2)$ hence our five standard normals can be use to create the desired properties: $.8 + 5(-1.7) = -7.7$, $.8 + 5(.55) = 3.55$, $.8 + 5(-.3) = -0.7$, $.8 + 5(-.02) = .7$, and $.8 + 5(.85) = 5.05$.

Question 18.4.

Sums and differences of two random variables are normally distributed hence $x_1 + x_2$ is normally distributed with mean $\mu_1 + \mu_2 = 10$ and variance

$$\sigma_1^2 + \sigma_2^2 + 2\rho\sigma_1\sigma_2 = 0.5 + 14 + \left[2 \times (-0.3) \times \sqrt{0.5 \times 14}\right] = 10.3$$

The difference is normally distributed with mean $\mu_1 - \mu_2 = -6$ and (higher) variance

$$\sigma_1^2 + \sigma_2^2 - 2\rho\sigma_1\sigma_2 = 0.5 + 14 - \left[2 \times (-0.3) \times \sqrt{0.5 \times 14}\right] = 18.7.$$

Question 18.6.

If $x \sim \mathcal{N}(\mu, \sigma^2)$ then $E(e^x) = ex^{\mu + .5\sigma^2}$; using the given numbers, $E(e^x) = e^{2+2.5} = 90.017$. There is a 50% probability x is below its mean of 2 hence the median of e^x is $e^2 = 7.3891$.

Question 18.8.

Since $S_t = S_0 \exp\left(\left(\alpha - \frac{1}{2}\sigma^2\right)t + \sigma\sqrt{t}z\right)$ where z is standard normal,

$$P(S_t > 105) = P\left(\left(\alpha - \frac{1}{2}\sigma^2\right)t + \sigma\sqrt{t}z > \ln\left(\frac{105}{100}\right)\right)$$

$$= P\left(z > \frac{\ln\left(\frac{105}{100}\right) - \left(\alpha - \frac{1}{2}\sigma^2\right)t}{\sigma\sqrt{t}}\right)$$

$$= P\left(-z < \frac{-\ln\left(\frac{105}{100}\right) + \left(\alpha - \frac{1}{2}\sigma^2\right)t}{\sigma\sqrt{t}}\right) = N(d_2)$$

where $d_2 = \left[\ln(100/105) + \left(\alpha - \frac{1}{2}\sigma^2\right)t\right] / \left(\sigma\sqrt{t}\right)$. Using the given parameters, $d_2 = .045967$ and $N(d_2) = .4817$. For this parameter specification, the probability $S_t > 105$ increases with t and decreases with σ. Analytically, since $N'(d_2) > 0$, the derivative will have the same sign as $\partial d_2 / \partial t$ and $\partial d_2 / \partial \sigma$. Specifically,

$$\frac{\partial P(S_t > K)}{\partial t} = N'(d_2) \frac{(\alpha - \sigma^2/2) - \ln(S_0/K)/t}{2\sigma\sqrt{t}} > 0$$

since $\alpha - \sigma^2/2 = .035 > 0$ and $\ln(S_0/K) < 0$. As an example, if t is 5 years, there is a 57.46% chance of being greater than 105. For volatility, let $t = 1$. Then

$$\frac{\partial P(S_t > K)}{\partial \sigma} = -N'(d_2)\left(\frac{\alpha - \ln(S_0/K)}{2\sigma^2} + \frac{1}{4}\right) < 0.$$

Question 18.10.

We have

$$P(S_t < 98) = P\left(\left(\alpha - \frac{1}{2}\sigma^2\right)t + \sigma\sqrt{t}z < \ln\left(\frac{98}{100}\right)\right)$$

$$= P\left(z < \frac{\ln\left(\frac{98}{100}\right) - \left(\alpha - \frac{1}{2}\sigma^2\right)t}{\sigma\sqrt{t}}\right) = N(-d_2)$$

with $-d_2 = (\ln(98/100) - .035)/.3 = -.18401$. Hence $P(S_t < 98) = N(-.18401) = 42.70\%$.

Question 18.12.

See Figure Two on the next page. Option prices depend on the conditional (risk neutral) expectation, not the probability the option is in the money. As T increases, the likelihood that $S_T > K_T$ may be lower; however, the payoff depends on the conditional expectation (since the option does not pay a constant amount). The increased dispersion offsets the lower probability (for the call option).

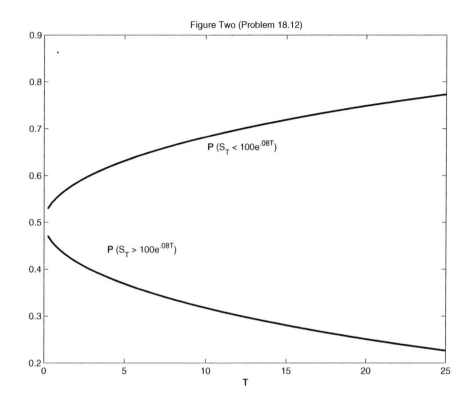

Figure Two (Problem 18.12)

Question 18.14.

The mean should be varying year by year; whereas, the standard deviation should be more stable.

Chapter 19
Monte Carlo Valuation

Question 19.2.

The histogram should be similar to a standard normal density ("bell" shaped). Since a uniform distribution has a mean of 0.5 and a variance of 1/12, the mean of $\sum_{i=1}^{12} u_i - 6$ is zero and the variance (& standard deviation) will be one since

$$var\left(\sum_{i=1}^{12} u_i\right) = 12var\left(u_i\right) = 1.$$

Question 19.4.

The standard deviation of the estimate will be $s_n/\sqrt{n}$ where s_n is the sample standard deviation of the n simulations. Since s_n is close to 2.9, $n = 84000$ should give a standard error close to 0.01.

Question 19.6.

The simulations should be generated by $S_1 = 100 \exp\left(.06 - .4^2/2 + .4z\right)$ where z is standard normal. The claim prices should be $e^{-.06}\overline{S^\alpha}$ where α is the relevant power and the $\overline{S^\alpha}$ is the average from the simulations. These values should be close to

$$100^\alpha \exp\left((\alpha - 1)\left(.06 + \frac{\alpha}{2}.4^2\right)\right).$$

Using this, the three values should be close to 12461, 9.51, and .000135 respectively.

Question 19.8.

By log normality

$$P\left(S_t < 95\right) = P\left(100 \exp\left(\left(.1 - .2^2/2\right)t + .2\sqrt{t}z\right) < 95\right)$$

$$P\left(z < \frac{\ln\left(95/100\right) - \left(.1 - .2^2/2\right)t}{.2\sqrt{t}}\right)$$

with $t = 1/365$ this is $N\left(-4.9207\right) = 4 \times 10^{-7}$. This magnitude negative return should, on average, occur once every 2.5 million days. With $t = 1/252$ (i.e. one trading day) this becomes $N\left(-4.0965\right) = 2.097 \times 10^{-5}$; making such a drop is similarly unlikely.

Question 19.10.

The simulations should be done by generating 1000 standard normals ε_1 and another 1000 (independent) standard normals ε_2. Then let $S_1 = 40 \exp\left(\frac{.08-.3/2}{12} + \frac{.3}{\sqrt{12}}\varepsilon_1\right)$ and let $S_2 = 100 \exp\left(\frac{.08-.5/2}{12} + \frac{.5}{\sqrt{12}}z\right)$ where $z = .45\varepsilon_1 + \sqrt{1 - .45^2}\varepsilon_2$. The means, standard deviations, and correlation from Monte Carlo should approximate their theoretical counterparts.

Question 19.12.

See Table One for a typical simulation. With weekly data, the lognormality (as opposed to normal) of the stock price isn't strong (i.e. there is little skewness or kurtosis). This implies the simple return is not that different from the continuous (normal) return. However, when we look at yearly distributions, there is now significant kurtosis and skewness.

TABLE ONE (Problem 19.12)

	Returns		Stock Price	
	Week	Year	Week	Year
Mean	0.0030	0.1551	100.3862	122.1316
SD	0.0415	0.2995	4.1708	37.4255
Skewness	0.0013	0.0013	0.1267	0.9511
Kurtosis	3.0133	3.0133	3.0390	4.6230

Question 19.14.

Using simple gross returns (i.e. $Payoff/Cost$), the mean should be around 1.62, the standard deviation around 1.49, skewness around 1.79, and kurtosis around 7.59.

Question 19.16.

We can write down the optimal exercise schedule based on our results in exercise 19.15.

Path	t=1	t=2	t=3
1	0	0	0
2	0	0	0
3	0	0	1
4	1	0	0
5	0	0	0
6	1	0	0
7	1	0	0
8	1	0	0

The cash flows associated with this exercise schedule are:

Path	t=1	t=2	t=3
1	0	0	0
2	0	0	0
3	0	0	0.07
4	0.17	0	0
5	0	0	0
6	0.34	0	0
7	0.18	0	0
8	0.22	0	0

At $t = 0$, we therefore have the following continuation values

pv (continuation)

0
0
0.058468915
0.160099971
0
0.320199941
0.169517616
0.207188197

At $t = 0$, we can just estimate a regression with a constant, because the stock price and the squared stock price are constant and equal to one. All paths have an immediate exercise value of $1.1 - 1 = 0.1$, and thus need to be included in the regression. The coefficient on the constant of this regression is 0.114. This is larger than the intrinsic value of 0.1, therefore early exercise in never optimal in $t = 0$.

Hence, we can find the value of the American put option to be:

$$
\begin{array}{l}
0 \\
0 \\
0.058468915 \\
0.160099971 \\
0 \\
0.320199941 \\
0.169517616 \\
0.207188197 \\
\hline
\mathbf{0.11443433} \quad = \textbf{average(values above)}
\end{array}
$$

For the European put option, we take the payoffs at $t = 3$, discount them at the risk-free rate, and then average the payoffs. We have:

Discounted Payoff	Payoff t=3
0	0
0	0
0.058468915	0.07
0.150348638	0.18
0	0
0.167054042	0.2
0.075174319	0.09
0	0
0.056380739	**= average()**

Chapter 20
Brownian Motion and Itô's Lemma

Question 20.2.

If $y = S^2$ then $S = \sqrt{y}$ and $dy = \left(2S\alpha\,(S,t) + \sigma\,(S,t)^2\right)dt + 2S\sigma\,(S,t)\,dZ_t$ where $\alpha\,(S,t)$ is the drift of S and $\sigma\,(S,t)$ is the volatility of S. For the three specifications:

a) $dy = \left(2\alpha\sqrt{y} + \sigma^2\right)dt + 2\sqrt{y}\sigma\,dZ_t.$

b)

$$dy = \left(2\sqrt{y}\lambda\,\left(a - \sqrt{y}\right) + \sigma^2\right)dt + 2\sqrt{y}\sigma\,dZ_t \qquad (1)$$

$$= \left(2\lambda a\sqrt{y} - 2\lambda y + \sigma^2\right)dt + 2\sqrt{y}\sigma\,dZ_t. \qquad (2)$$

c) $dy = \left(2\alpha + \sigma^2\right)y\,dt + 2\sigma y\,dZ_t.$

Question 20.4.

If $y = \sqrt{S}$ then $S = y^2$ and

$$dy = \left(\frac{1}{2}S^{-1/2}\alpha\,(S,t) - \frac{1}{8}S^{-3/2}\sigma\,(S,t)^2\right)dt + \frac{1}{2}S^{-1/2}\sigma\,(S,t)\,dZ_t \qquad (3)$$

$$= \left(\frac{1}{2y}\alpha\,(S,t) - \frac{1}{8y^3}\sigma\,(S,t)^2\right)dt + \frac{1}{2y}\sigma\,(S,t)\,dZ_t \qquad (4)$$

a) $dy = \left(\frac{\alpha}{2y} - \frac{\sigma^2}{8y^3}\right)dt + \frac{\sigma}{2y}dZ_t.$

b) $dy = \left(\frac{\lambda a}{2y} - \frac{\lambda}{2y^2} - \frac{\sigma^2}{8y^3}\right)dt + \frac{\sigma}{2y}dZ_t.$

c) $dy = \left(\frac{\alpha}{2} - \frac{\sigma^2}{8}\right)y\,dt + \frac{\sigma}{2}y\,dZ_t.$

Question 20.6.

If $y = \ln(SQ) = \ln(S) + \ln(Q)$ then

$$dy = d\ln(S) + d\ln(Q) \tag{5}$$

$$= \left(\alpha_S - \delta_S - \sigma_S^2/2 + \alpha_Q - \delta_Q - \sigma_Q^2/2\right) dt + \sigma_S dZ_S + \sigma_Q dZ_Q. \tag{6}$$

Question 20.8.

Since the process $y = S^a Q^b$ follows geometric Brownian motion, i.e. $dy = \alpha_y y dt + \sigma_y y dZ_y$ the price of the claims will be $e^{-r} E^*(y_1) = y_0 e^{(\alpha_y - r)}$. We use Ito's lemma, as in equation (20.38), with $\delta = 0$ and $\alpha_S = \alpha_Q = r$ to arrive at the drift

$$\alpha_y = ar + br + \frac{1}{2}a(a-1)\sigma_S^2 + \frac{1}{2}b(b-1)\sigma_Q^2 + ab\rho\sigma_S\sigma_Q \tag{7}$$

$$= .06(a+b) + \frac{.4^2}{2}a(a-1) + \frac{.2^2}{2}b(b-1) - .3(.4)(.2)ab. \tag{8}$$

a)   Since $a = b = 1$, $y_0 = 10000$ and $\alpha_y = .12 - .024 = .096$ hence the claim is worth $10000e^{.096-.06} = 10366.56$.

b)   Since $a = 1$ and $b = -1$, $y_0 = 1$ and $\alpha_y = .2^2 + .024 = .064$ hence the claim is worth $e^{.064-.06} = 1.004$.

c)   Since $a = 1/2$ and $b = 1/2$, $y_0 = 100$ and $\alpha_y = .029$ hence the claim is worth $100e^{.029-.06} = 96.948$.

d)   Since $a = -1$ and $b = -1$, $y_0 = 1/10000$ and $\alpha_y = .056$ hence the claim is worth $\left(e^{.056-.06}\right)/10000 = 9.9601 \times 10^{-5}$.

e)   Since $a = 2$ and $b = 1$, $y_0 = 1000000$ and $\alpha_y = .292$ hence the claim is worth $1000000e^{.292-.06} = 1.2612$ million.

Question 20.10.

Note that if $V(S)$ satisfies the given equation, then

$$E^*(dV) = \left[(r-\delta)SV_S + \frac{1}{2}\sigma^2 S^2 V_{SS}\right] dt = rV dt. \tag{9}$$

Since $V(S) = kS^{h_1}$ where a is constant, showing $y = S^a$ satisfies $E^*(dy) = ry dt$ when $a = h_1$ is

137

sufficient (i.e. the constant term is irrelevant). Using Ito's lemma,

$$E^* (dy) = aS^{a-1} (r - \delta) S + \frac{1}{2} a (a - 1) S^{a-2} \sigma^2 S^2 \tag{10}$$

$$= \left(a (r - \delta) y + a (a - 1) \frac{\sigma^2}{2} y \right) dt. \tag{11}$$

If $E^* (dy) = r y dt$ then a must satisfy

$$a (r - \delta) + a (a - 1) \frac{\sigma^2}{2} = r. \tag{12}$$

The two solutions are h_1 and h_2 as given (12.11) and (12.12) which one can verify directly.

Question 20.12.

We must try to find a position in S and Q that eliminates risk. Let us buy one unit of S and let θ be the position in Q. Let I_t be our bond investment. We have $V_t = S_t + \theta_t Q_t + I_t$ with $V_0 = 0$. Since this strategy must be self financing,

$$dV = \left(\alpha_S S + \theta \alpha_Q Q + rI \right) dt + (\sigma_S S - \eta \theta Q) dZ \tag{13}$$

hence we will set $\theta = \sigma_S S / (\eta Q)$. This will make our zero cost, self financing strategy riskless. Hence the drift and the value must be zero. Mathematically, if $V_t = 0$ then $I = -S - \frac{\sigma_S S}{\eta Q} Q$. The drift being zero implies

$$\alpha_S S + \frac{\sigma_S S}{\eta Q} \alpha_Q Q - r \left(S + \frac{\sigma_S S}{\eta} \right) = 0. \tag{14}$$

Dividing both sides by S and simplifying leads to

$$\alpha_Q = r - \frac{\alpha_S - r}{\sigma_S} \eta. \tag{15}$$

Since Q is negatively related to Z, if S has a positive risk premium then Q will negative risk premium.

Question 20.14.

As mentioned in the problem, σdZ appears in both dS and dQ. One can think of dQ as an alternative model for the stock (with dS being the standard geometric Brownian motion).

a)   If there were no jumps, dQ would also be geometric Brownian motion. Since it has the same risk component, σdZ, α_Q must equal α. If we thought of Q as another traded asset, this naturally follows from no arbitrage.

b)   If $Y_1 > 1$ then there are only positive jumps. We would therefore expect $\alpha_Q < \alpha$ to compensate for this. Mathematically, $dQ/Q - dS/S = (\alpha_Q - \alpha) \, dt + dq_1$. If a jump occurs, $dq_1 = Y_1 - 1 > 0$; if $\alpha_Q \geq \alpha$ we could buy Q and short S. The only risk we have is jump risk but this will always be "good" news for our portfolio. In order to avoid this arbitrage α_Q must be less than α.

If we use a weaker assumption $k_1 = E(Y_1 - 1) > 0$ and we assume the returns to S and Q should be the same (this makes sense if we are looking at Q as an alternative model instead of another stock) then we arrive at a similar result. The expected return to Q is $\alpha_Q + \lambda_1 k_1$; setting this equal to α implies $\alpha - \alpha_Q = \lambda_1 k_1 > 0$.

c)   Let α^* be the expected return of Q. Note that α_Q is not the expected return, it is the expected return conditional on no jumps occurring. We have the following relationship,

$$\alpha^* = E\left(\frac{dQ}{Q}\right)/dt = \alpha_Q + k_1\lambda_1 + k_2\lambda_2 \tag{16}$$

where $k_i = E(Y_i - 1)$. Hence $\alpha_Q = \alpha^* - k_1\lambda_1 - k_2\lambda_2$. If $\alpha^* = \alpha$ (i.e. Q and S have the same expected return) then $\alpha - \alpha_Q = k_1\lambda_1 + k_2\lambda_2$. The sign of which could be positive or negative if there are no restriction on k_1 and k_2.

Chapter 21
The Black-Scholes Equation

Question 21.2.

If $V(S,t) = AS^a e^{\gamma t}$ then $V_t = \gamma V$, $V_S = aS^{a-1}e^{\gamma t} = aV/S$, and $V_{SS} = a(a-1)S^{a-2}e^{\gamma t} = a(a-1)V/S^2$. Therefore the left hand side of the Black-Scholes equation (21.11) is

$$V_t + (r-\delta)V_S S + V_{SS}S^2\sigma^2/2 - rV = \left(\gamma - r + (r-\delta)a + \frac{\sigma^2}{2}a(a-1)\right)V. \qquad (1)$$

We can rewrite the coefficient of V as

$$\gamma + (r-\delta)a + \frac{\sigma^2}{2}a(a-1) = \frac{\sigma^2}{2}a^2 + \left(r-\delta-\frac{\sigma^2}{2}\right)a + \gamma - r. \qquad (2)$$

From the quadratic formula, this has roots

$$a = \frac{-\left(r-\delta-\frac{\sigma^2}{2}\right)}{\sigma^2} \pm \frac{\sqrt{\left(r-\delta-\frac{\sigma^2}{2}\right)^2 - 4\frac{\sigma^2}{2}(\gamma - r)}}{\sigma^2}. \qquad (3)$$

Simplifying,

$$a = \left(\frac{1}{2} - \frac{r-\delta}{\sigma^2}\right) \pm \sqrt{\left(\frac{r-\delta}{\sigma^2} - \frac{1}{2}\right)^2 + \frac{2(r-\gamma)}{\sigma^2}}. \qquad (4)$$

Note, for a given γ, these are the only values for a that will satisfy the PDE.

Question 21.4.

Defining $V(S,t) = Ke^{-r(T-t)} + Se^{-\delta(T-t)}$ we have $V_t = rKe^{-r(T-t)} + \delta Se^{-\delta(T-t)}$, $V_S = e^{-\delta(T-t)}$ and $V_{SS} = 0$. The Black-Scholes equation is satisfied for $V_t + (r-\delta)V_S S + V_{SS}S^2\sigma^2/2$ is

$$rKe^{-r(T-t)} + \delta Se^{-\delta(T-t)} + (r-\delta)e^{-\delta(T-t)}S \qquad (5)$$

$$= r\left(Ke^{-r(T-t)} + Se^{-\delta(T-t)}\right) = rV. \qquad (6)$$

This also follows from the result that linear combinations of solutions of the PDE are also solutions. The boundary condition is $V(S,T) = K + S_T$, i.e. we receive one share and K dollars. Similarly, a long forward contract with value $Se^{-\delta(T-t)} - Ke^{-r(T-t)}$ will solve the PDE.

Question 21.6.

Let $V(S,t) = e^{-r(T-t)}N(d_2)$; we must show V solves the PDE $V_t + (r-\delta)SV_S + S^2\sigma^2 V_{SS}/2 = rV$. Note that

$$d_2 = \frac{\ln(S/K)}{\sigma\sqrt{T-t}} + \left(\frac{r-\delta-\sigma^2/2}{\sigma}\right)\sqrt{T-t} \tag{7}$$

depends on both S and t. Beginning with the first term in the PDE,

$$V_t = rV + e^{-r(T-t)}N'(d_2)\left(\frac{\ln(S/K)}{2\sigma(T-t)^{3/2}} - \frac{r-\delta-\sigma^2/2}{2\sigma(T-t)^{1/2}}\right)$$

$$= rV + \frac{e^{-r(T-t)}N'(d_2)}{2(T-t)}\left(d_2 - \frac{2(r-\delta-\sigma^2/2)}{\sigma}\sqrt{T-t}\right). \tag{8}$$

Since $V_S = e^{-r(T-t)}N'(d_2)/\left(S\sigma\sqrt{T-t}\right)$ the second term in the PDE is

$$(r-\delta)SV_S = \left(\frac{r-\delta}{\sigma\sqrt{T-t}}\right)e^{-r(T-t)}N'(d_2). \tag{9}$$

The second partial of V with respect to S is

$$V_{SS} = \frac{e^{-r(T-t)}\left(N''(d_2) - N'(d_2)\right)}{S^2\sigma^2(T-t)} = -\frac{e^{-r(T-t)}N'(d_2)}{S^2\sigma^2(T-t)}\left(d_2 + \sigma\sqrt{T-t}\right) \tag{10}$$

where we use the property $N''(x) = -xN'(x)$. The third term in the PDE is therefore

$$\frac{S^2\sigma^2 V_{SS}}{2} = -\frac{e^{-r(T-t)}N'(d_2)}{2(T-t)}\left(d_2 + \sigma\sqrt{T-t}\right). \tag{11}$$

Adding equations (8), (9), and (11), all terms cancel expect the rV term in equation (8); i.e. V satisfies the PDE.

Question 21.8.

These bets are all or nothing options. The cash bets being worth, per dollar, $e^{-rT}N(d_2)$ if we receive $1 if $S_T > K$ and $e^{-rT}N(-d_2)$ if we receive $1 if $S_T < K$. The stock bets being worth, per share, $SN(d_1)$ if we receive 1 share if $S_T > K$ and $SN(-d_1)$ if we receive 1 share if $S_T < K$. (Note we are assuming the current time is $t = 0$ and the bet is for the stock price T years from now).

a)   By setting $K = Se^{(r-\delta)T}$, $d_2 = -\sigma\sqrt{T}/2$ the value of the bet that the share price will exceed the forward price is $e^{-rT}N(-\sigma\sqrt{T}/2)$. This is always less than the opposite bet, which has value $e^{-rT}N(\sigma\sqrt{T}/2)$.

b)   If denominated in cash, we could make the bet fair by setting the strike price equal to $K = Se^{(r-\delta-.5\sigma^2)T}$, which is the median (50% of the probability is above this value). This will make $d_2 = 0$ and the bets worth $e^{-rT}/2$ which is not a surprise since the sum of the two bets must be worth e^{-rT}. Using $T = 1, r = 6\%, \sigma = 30\%$, we have $K = 100e^{.06-.3^2/2} = 101.51$.

c)   If denominated in shares, we could make the bet fair by setting the strike price equal to $K = Se^{(r-\delta+.5\sigma^2)T} = 100e^{.06+.3^2/2} = 111.07$, which is above the forward price. This makes $d_1 = 0$ and the bets worth $S/2 = 50$.

Question 21.10.

If we purchase one unit of the claim, $-V_S$ shares, and invest W in the risk free bond, our investment is worth $I = V(S, t) - V_S S + W = 0$. By purchasing one claim, we will receive a dividend of Γdt that will be added to dI. The change in the investment value is

$$dI = \Gamma dt + V_t dt + V_S dS + \frac{\sigma^2 S^2 V_{SS} dt}{2} - V_S dS - V_S \delta S dt + rW dt \qquad (12)$$

$$= \left(\Gamma + V_t + \frac{1}{2}\sigma^2 S^2 V_{SS} - V_S \delta S + rW \right) dt. \qquad (13)$$

Since this is risk free and is (initially) a zero investment, both the drift and I must be zero. This implies $W = V_S S - V$ and

$$\Gamma + V_t + \frac{1}{2}\sigma^2 S^2 V_{SS} - V_S \delta S + r (V_S S - V) = 0, \qquad (14)$$

hence

$$\Gamma + V_t + \frac{1}{2}\sigma^2 S^2 V_{SS} + (r - \delta) V_S S = rV. \qquad (15)$$

Note that if we assume Γ is a continuous yield of the claim (rather than a $ per unit rate), the first term would be ΓV rather than Γ.

Question 21.12.

Setting $b = -1$ and using Proposition 21.1, we change the dividend yield of S to $\eta = .02 - .2(.3)(.5) = -.01$. The prepaid forward price, i.e. V in equation (21.35), is $S_0 e^{-\eta T}$. Letting $\delta^* = .06 + (.06 - .01) - .5^2 = -.14$, we have the value of the claim being

$$\frac{1}{90}e^{.2(2)} \left(50e^{.01(2)} \right) = 0.8455. \qquad (16)$$

Using Proposition 20.4, the claim should be worth

$$S_0 e^{-\delta T} \left(Q_0^b e^{\left(b(r - \delta_Q) + .5b(b-1)\sigma_Q^2 \right)2} \right) e^{b\rho\sigma\sigma_Q T} \tag{17}$$

which equals

$$50 e^{-.04} \left(90^{-1} e^{(-.05 + .5^2)2} \right) e^{.03(2)} = 0.8455. \tag{18}$$

Note that Proposition 20.4 derives the forward price; upon discounting, the forward price of S becomes $S_0 e^{-\delta T}$ and the forward price of Q^b terms does not get discounted.

Question 21.14.

Using Proposition 21.1, since $b = 1$, the insurance payoff should be worth

$$Q e^{(r - \delta_Q)T} V (S, K, \sigma_S, r, T, \delta - \rho\sigma\sigma_S) \tag{19}$$

hence we should use a dividend yield of $.02 + .2 (.3) (.5) = .05$ making the put relatively more valuable. For $K = 50$, $V = 7.09$ hence the insurance is worth $90 e^{(.06 - .01)2} (7.09) = 705.21$. If we wanted to insure $90 e^{(.06 - .01)2} = 99.465$ units, it would cost $90 e^{(.06 - .01)2} (6.05) = 601.77$. This is intuitive since $\ln (S)$ and $\ln (Q)$ are negatively correlated. When Q is high, S is more likely to be low making the insurance payout larger (the holder has the right to sell *more* units for K).

Chapter 22
Exotic Options: II

Question 22.2.

In the same way as the COD, the paylater is priced initially using

$$0 = BSPut(S_0, K, \sigma, r, T, \delta) - P \times DR(S_0, K, \sigma, r, T, \delta, H).$$

Thus, the amount to be paid if the barrier is hit is

$$P = \frac{BSPut(S_0, K, \sigma, r, T, \delta)}{DR(S_0, K, \sigma, r, T, \delta, H)} = \frac{2.3101}{0.7590} = 3.0436.$$

At subsequent times prior to hitting the barrier, the value of the paylater put is

$$BSPut(S_0, K, \sigma, r, T - t, \delta) - P \times DR(S_0, K, \sigma, r, T - t, \delta, H)$$

The paylater premium has the potential to be much lower than the COD premium. Compare a paylater with $H = K$ to a COD. You'll find in many cases that the COD premium is approximately twice as great. This is a consequence of the reflection principle—once you have hit the barrier, there is approximately a 50% chance that the option will move out of the money, which means that half the time, you'll pay the premium without the option paying off. Thus, the premium is half that of the COD, where the premium is always paid when and only when the option is in the money.

The initial delta will be $-.1903 - 3.0436\,(-.0439) = -0.0567$. The DR has a gamma very close to zero hence, initially, there is little difference between the paylater's gamma and a regular put option's gamma.

As time evolves the behavior of delta and gamma becomes similar to the COD, since in each case a small move can trigger a discrete payment; the main difference being that the discrete payment is likely to occur before expiration when S_t gets close to the barrier.

Question 22.4.

We must show the formula is a solution to $e^{-r(T-t)} P\left(\overline{S}_T \geq H \text{ and } S_T < K\right)$ where P stands for risk neutral probability.

We begin with the case when $H \geq K$ (i.e. the top equation). If the barrier is hit, i.e. $S = H$, $-d_4 = -d_2$ implying the probability is $N(-d_2) = P(S_T < K)$ (i.e. the risk neutral probability of receiving one dollar). If at time T, $\overline{S}_T \geq H$ and $S_T < K$, the barrier has been hit and the probability is equal to $N(-d_2) = 1$. Lastly, if at time T, $\overline{S}_T < H$ or $S_T > K$ we must check the probability is zero. If $S_T > K$ and the barrier has been hit, the probability becomes $N(-d_2) = 0$. If the barrier has not been hit (as a reminder $S_T > K$), then $S_T < H$ and $H^2/(S_T K) > 0$ implying $d_4 \to \infty$. The probability will be $\left(\frac{H}{S}\right)^k N(-d_4) = 0$.

For the case when $H < K$, if the barrier is hit $d_6 = d_8$ and H drops out of the probability leaving $N(-d_2) = P(S_T < K)$. If at time T, $\overline{S}_T \geq H$ and $S_T < K$, the barrier has been hit and the probability is equal to $N(-d_2) = 1$. Finally, if at time T, $\overline{S}_T < H$ or $S_T > K$ we must check the probability is zero. If $S_T > K$ the barrier must have been hit and the probability is $N(-d_2) = 0$. If the barrier has not been hit, i.e. $\overline{S}_T < H$, then $S_T < H < K$. In this case $d_2 = d_6$ and $-d_8 = -\infty$ implying the probability equals zero.

Question 22.6.

Equivalently, we could use $x_0 Q_0 = 200$ as the stock price and set the dividend yield equal to $\delta_Q + \rho s \sigma_Q + r - r_f$. This gives $BSCall(200, 195, .15, .08, 1, .02 + .2 \times .1 \times .15 + .08 - .04) = \$15.319$.

Question 22.8.

The two \$ traded assets are Y and x. Applying Proposition 20.4 to these ratio of these two yields

$$F_{t,T}\left(\frac{Y}{x}\right) = F_{t,T}(Y) \, F_{t,T}\left(\frac{1}{x}\right) e^{-\rho \sigma_{YS}(T-t)}. \tag{1}$$

Note that ρ is the correlation between Y and $1/x$ which implies $\rho \sigma_{YS}$ is the covariance given by equation (22.28). Since the forward price for Y is $Y_t e^{(r-\delta_Q)(T-t)}$ and the forward price for $(1/x)$ is $(1/x_t) e^{(r_f - r + s^2)(T-t)}$ we have

$$F_{t,T}\left(\frac{Y}{x}\right) = Q_t e^{(r-\delta_Q + r_f - r + s^2 - \rho s \sigma_Q - s^2)(T-t)} = Q_t e^{(r_f - \delta_Q - \rho s \sigma_Q)(T-t)}. \tag{2}$$

The prepaid forward price is therefore $Q_t e^{(r_f - \delta_Q - \rho s \sigma_Q - r)(T-t)}$.

Question 22.10.

The value of the option is going to depend upon the probability that the stock at expiration will be greater than K, conditional on it having exceeded H_1 without ever having exceeded H_2.

One way to value an option like this is to use Monte Carlo simulation. By simulating the path of the stock price, we can isolate those paths along which we hit H_1 without hitting H_2.

However, we can also view this relatively complicated option as a *spread* of barrier options. Consider the following strategy:

•Buy an ordinary knock-in call with strike K and barrier H_1

•Write an ordinary knock-in call with strike K and barrier H_2

Now consider the payoffs given the different possible combinations of the stock hitting or not hitting the two barriers:

Payoff	H_1 not hit	H_1 hit	
		H_2 not hit	H_2 hit
Purchased knock-in	0	$Max(0, S_T - K)$	$Max(0, S_T - K)$
Written knock-in	0	0	$-Max(0, S_T - K)$
Total	0	$Max(0, S_T - K)$	0

By entering into a knock-in spread, we are able to replicate the payoff to the knock-in, knock-out.[1]

Question 22.12.

a)   If we plan to buy back the option at a predetermined stock price, we could implement this strategy mechanically by buying a knock-in call which knocks-in at the buy-back stock price. The buy-back price is the barrier. Thus, if we write a call intending to buy it back at a certain stock price, we have really written a knock-out call.

b)   The knock-in call that we will buy at $45 to offset the written call has a premium

$$CallDownIn(50, 50, .3, .08, 1, 0, 45) = \$2.595$$

Thus, the net premium raised by selling the call in the first place is $\$7.856 - \$2.595 = \$5.261$.

The use of a barrier option automatically offsets our written call position if the stock price hits the barrier. Thinking about the strategy this way has the benefit that we can determine *from the outset* the net premium we receive from writing the call: it is the call premium less the cost of the knock-in call.

Question 22.14.

When using equation (22.52) for the lookback put, $\widetilde{S}_t = \overline{S}_t$ and $\omega = -1$.

a)   If the stock is worthless the put will be exercised at time T and the holder will sell a worthless stock for $\overline{S}$ (which is known). This implies the lookback put should be worth the present value of $\overline{S}$. To verify, if $S_t = 0$, $\overline{S}$ will be greater than S and the first term in equation (22.52) will be zero (since the term in brackets is bounded). The second term is $\overline{S}e^{-r(T-t)}N\left(-d_6'\right)$. Since $S = 0$ and $\overline{S} > 0$, $d_6' \to -\infty$ implying $N\left(-d_6'\right) \to 1$ and the lookback put is worth $\overline{S}e^{-r(T-t)}$.

---

[1]The easy pricing formula in this example relied on the fact that the knock-out price exceeded the knock-in price. There are also knock-in knock-out options for which the stock price is *between* the knock-in and knock-out prices. For example if the current stock price is 100 we might have an option which knocks in at 80 and then knocks out at 120. These are not priced so easily, since we might hit the knock-out price before the option has knocked in. Numerical methods are required to price these options.

b)   At maturity if $S_T < \overline{S}_T$ then each $d_5' \to -\infty$ which implies $N\left(d_5'\right) \to 0$ and both $N\left(-d_5'\right)$ and $N\left(d_6'\right) \to 1$. Similarly $d_8' \to \infty$, implying $N\left(-d_8'\right) \to 0$. As a reminder $\omega = -1$; hence equation (22.52) becomes

$$-S_T\,(1-0) + \overline{S}_T\,(1-0) = \overline{S}_T - S_T. \tag{3}$$

If we happen to have $S_T = \underline{S}_T$, then each $d_i = 0$ and equation (22.52) becomes

$$-S_T\left(\frac{1}{2} - \frac{\sigma^2}{4\,(r-\delta)}\right) + \overline{S}_T\left(\left(\frac{1}{2} - \frac{\sigma^2}{4\,(r-\delta)}\right)\right) = 0. \tag{4}$$

Question 22.16.

Let $y_t \equiv Q_0 \times S_t / Q_t$. If exercised, the option pays off

$$\left(S_t - S_0 \frac{Q_t}{Q_0}\right)^+ m\left(\frac{S_t/S_0}{Q_t/Q_0}\right). \tag{5}$$

where $m\,(\cdot)$ is the multiplier. We can rewrite the payoff as

$$\frac{Q_t}{Q_0}\,(y_t - S_0)^+\, m\,(y_t) = \frac{Q_t}{Q_0} f\,(y_t). \tag{6}$$

As in the exchange option, we can use Proposition 21.1 to value the y payoff using a dividend yield of $r - \delta_Q$ and a volatility of $\sqrt{\sigma^2 + \sigma_Q^2 - 2\rho\sigma\sigma_Q}$. This can be done with the binomial model with an "interest rate" of δ_Q since the risk neutral probability is

$$\frac{e^{(r-(r-\delta_Q))\Delta t} - d}{u - d} = \frac{e^{\delta_Q \Delta t} - d}{u - d}. \tag{7}$$

Let $V\,(y_t)$ be this value, then Proposition 21.1 implies the Level 3 outperformance option will have a value of

$$\frac{Q_t e^{(r-\delta_Q)(T-t)}}{Q_0} V\,(y_t). \tag{8}$$

This implies the current value (i.e. $t = 0$) of the option is simply $V\,(y_0)$. To find terminal value of the option, i.e. $V\,(y_T)$, we have to use the multiplier. For example, if the terminal node is $y\,(T) = 300$ then Level 3 will have outperformed the S&P by an annualized rate of $3^{.25} - 1 = .3161$; since this is greater than 11%, we will receive a payoff of $(300 - 100) \times 8$. If the annualized rate is less than 11% (but greater than zero) we receive a payoff of $(y_T - 100) \times \frac{8}{11} \times 100$.

a)   See Table One for a 10 step binomial tree.

TABLE ONE (Problem 22.16a)

	0.4	0.8	1.2	1.6	2	2.4	2.8	3.2	3.6	4
Time (yrs)										
100	116.9995	136.8889	160.1594	187.3858	219.2405	256.5104	300.1161	351.1344	410.8257	480.6642
	240.7747	357.7046	515.7807	720.112	972.3534	1271.441	1618.023	2020.513	2492.345	3045.313
	86.7101	101.4504	118.6965	138.8744	162.4824	190.1037	222.4205	260.2309	304.469	356.2273
	88.3768	143.3498	226.4299	346.8114	512.6455	727.9501	990.1712	1293.285	1641.491	2049.819
Value		75.18641	87.96775	102.9219	120.4181	140.8887	164.8391	192.861	225.6465	264.0054
157.74		42.24001	73.75534	125.8406	208.7116	334.1874	511.9977	742.5413	1010.911	1312.043
European Call			65.19421	76.27692	89.24365	104.4147	122.1647	142.9321	167.2299	195.6583
Strike = 100			15.67706	29.90796	56.19063	103.4985	185.6077	320.4118	521.4917	765.2662
Vol = 23.69%; r = 1.80%				56.52996	66.13979	77.38326	90.53806	105.9291	123.9366	145.0052
Exp = 4 years; Div = 0.00%				3.636767	7.6839	16.21976	34.20409	72.05331	151.6146	318.6434
u = 1.170; d = 0.867					49.01718	57.34988	67.0991	78.50564	91.85124	107.4655
Risk-neutral prob of up = 0.463					0.201573	0.438869	0.955515	2.080367	4.52942	9.861551
						42.50284	49.72813	58.18169	68.07231	79.6443
						0	0	0	0	0
							36.85426	43.11931	50.4494	59.02557
							0	0	0	0
								31.95636	37.3888	43.74472
								0	0	0
									27.70939	32.41986
									0	0
										24.02684
										0

b)   See Table two for a 10 step binomial tree.

TABLE TWO (Problem 22.16b)

	0.4	0.8	1.2	1.6	2	2.4	2.8	3.2	3.6	4
Time (yrs)										
100	116.9995	136.8889	160.1594	187.3858	219.2405	256.5104	300.1161	351.1344	410.8257	480.6642
	240.8171	357.7704	515.8763	720.2369	972.4894	1271.539	1618.023	2020.513	2492.345	3045.313
	86.7101	101.4504	118.6965	138.8744	162.4824	190.1037	222.4205	260.2309	304.469	356.2273
	88.38895	143.3725	226.4711	346.8831	512.7625	728.12	990.3562	1293.285	1641.491	2049.819
Value		75.18641	87.96775	102.9219	120.4181	140.8887	164.8391	192.861	225.6465	264.0054
157.77		42.24326	73.76242	125.856	208.7452	334.2605	512.1566	(742.8879)	1010.911	1312.043
American Call			65.19421	76.27692	89.24365	104.4147	122.1647	142.9321	167.2299	195.6583
Strike = 100			15.67706	29.90796	56.19063	103.4985	185.6077	320.4118	521.4917	765.2662
Vol = 23.69%; r = 1.80%				56.52996	66.13979	77.38326	90.53806	105.9291	123.9366	145.0052
Exp = 4 years; Div = 0.00%				3.636767	7.6839	16.21976	34.20409	72.05331	151.6146	318.6434
u = 1.170; d = 0.867					49.01718	57.34988	67.0991	78.50564	91.85124	107.4655
Risk-neutral prob of up = 0.463					0.201573	0.438869	0.955515	2.080367	4.52942	9.861551
						42.50284	49.72813	58.18169	68.07231	79.6443
						0	0	0	0	0
							36.85426	43.11931	50.4494	59.02557
							0	0	0	0
								31.95636	37.3888	43.74472
								0	0	0
									27.70939	32.41986
									0	0
										24.02684
										0

c)   Notice early exercise in the middle of the American tree. If the option is deep in the money, standard arguments makes early exercise sub-optimal. We have a multiplier of 8 since there is a "cushion" (i.e. little risk of falling below the 11% cap). However, when we are just over the 11% cap, if the stock price falls we will lose out since the multiplier will fall. Since Level 3 pays no dividends, the multiplier is central to early exercise. If there was no multiplier there is no incentive to have early exercise since we essentially exchanging a dividend paying asset for a non-dividend paying asset.

Chapter 23
Volatility

Question 23.2.

	SP500	IBM	Xerox
12/31/1991	14.07%	24.02%	27.57%
12/31/1992	9.57%	27.80%	20.60%
12/31/1993	8.55%	29.54%	21.60%
12/30/1994	9.76%	29.58%	22.31%
12/29/1995	8.01%	23.21%	22.47%
12/31/1996	11.60%	33.58%	32.79%
12/31/1997	18.17%	35.03%	28.21%
12/31/1998	20.03%	30.23%	36.02%
12/31/1999	17.76%	41.94%	57.90%
12/29/2000	21.63%	48.21%	84.43%
12/31/2001	20.39%	35.38%	78.51%
12/31/2002	25.95%	42.41%	67.92%
12/31/2003	16.46%	22.38%	39.65%
12/31/2004	10.93%	14.42%	26.23%
Overall	**16.45%**	**32.91%**	**46.63%**

The results of the daily volatility calculations are remarkably similar to the weekly volatility calculations. We have the same time-series variation, and the magnitudes of most of the calculated volatilities are similar.

Question 23.4.

Here is the code you can use for a common statistical package, STATA:

```
Stata commands:

insheet using C:\garch_ibm.txt
tsset seqn
arch ret, arch(1/1) garch(1/1)
predict var, variance
```

This code produces the following results:

```
------------------------------------------------------------------------
        ret |     Coef.   Std. Err.      z    P>|z|    [ 95% Conf. Interval]
------------+-----------------------------------------------------------
ARCH        |
      arch  |
       B2.  |   .0440766   .0047828    9.22   0.000    .0347026   .0534507
     garch  |
       B3.  |   .9556661   .0053281  179.36   0.000    .9452231    .966109
       B1   |   1.34e-06   1.03e-06    1.30   0.193   -6.77e-07   3.36e-06
------------------------------------------------------------------------
```

You can see that the results are very close to the estimates reported in the book.

The following graph plots the annualized volatility based on the Garch (1,1) estimates—you should do this as well for your estimates of B1, B2, and B3, and compare it with the graph of the main textbook. They should look very similar.

Garch (1, 1) volatility for BM, Jan 1999 - Dec 2003

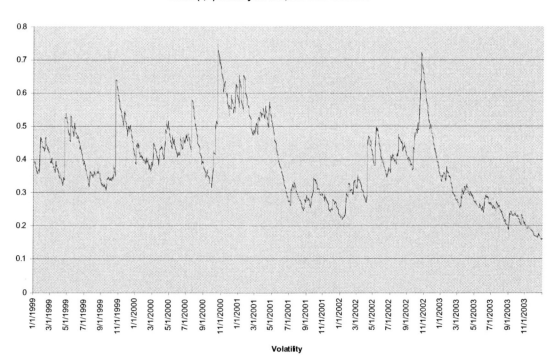

Volatility

If we exclude the four daily absolute returns above 12%, we obtain the following estimates:

```
------------------------------------------------------------------------
        ret |     Coef.   Std. Err.      z    P>|z|    [ 95% Conf. Interval]
------------+-----------------------------------------------------------
------------+-----------------------------------------------------------
ARCH        |
      arch  |
       B2.  |   .0472975   .0066992    7.06   0.000    .0341673   .0604277
     garch  |
       B3.  |   .9499507   .0075384  126.01   0.000    .9351757   .9647258
       B1   |   1.89e-06   1.26e-06    1.50   0.133   -5.73e-07   4.35e-06
------------------------------------------------------------------------
```

While the coefficients are a bit different from the ones in the book, we can calculate an unconditional volatility of:

$$\sqrt{\frac{0.00000189}{1 - 0.047295 - 0.9499507} \times 252} = 0.416,$$

which is very similar to the estimate of 0.4229 in the textbook.

Question 23.6.

Here is a table of volatilities and the corresponding option prices for the problem.

Volatility	Option Price
0.05	50.02999100179970
0.1	50.02999100179970
0.15	50.02999100179970
0.2	50.02999100179970
0.25	50.02999100179970
0.3	50.02999100179970
0.35	50.02999100179970
0.4	50.02999100179970
0.45	50.02999100179970
0.5	50.02999100179970
0.55	50.02999100179970
0.6	50.02999100179970
0.65	50.02999100179970
0.7	50.02999100179970
0.75	50.02999100179970
0.8	50.02999100179970
0.85	50.02999100179970
0.9	50.02999100179970
0.95	50.02999100179980
1	50.02999100180160
5	51.33309337854208

We can see that at a volatility of 30%, the option price is indeed 50.02999. The vega at a volatility of 30% is $2.129510350240270e - 116$, or virtually zero. Vega is measuring the sensitivity of the option price with respect to a change in the volatility. Note that we only have very little time left to maturity. Even if there is a lot of volatility, it will not be able to move the stock price significantly over such a short period of time. Only if we choose a very high volatility of 500%, we see that the stock price moves a significant amount.

This demonstrates that it is very difficult, if not impossible, to calculate implied volatilities for deep in-the-money call options with short maturities.

Question 23.8.

This is a snapshot from the excel spreadsheet:

Inputs		Black-Scholes (European)	Call	Put
Stock Price	50	Price	3E-119	49.94002
Exercise Price	100	Delta	4.6E-118	-1
Volatility	30.000%	Gamma	7.2E-117	7.2E-117
Risk-free interest rate	6.000%	Vega	5.4E-118	5.4E-118
Time to Expiration (years)	0.01	Theta	-2E-117	0.016428
Dividend Yield	0.000%	Rho	2.3E-120	-0.00999
# Binomial steps	4	Elasticity	772.8687	-1.0012
Type (0=Eur, 1=Amer)	0			

a) We can see from above that the price of the option is zero.

b) We can see from the spreadsheet that the vega is indeed zero. A small, local change in volatility does not have any impact on the option price, because the stock price needs to change by more than $50 in 0.01 years for the option to pay off a positive amount of money.

c) For the bid, we obtain an implied volatility of 29.94%, for the ask, we obtain an implied volatility of 285.25%. The logic behind the implied volatility for the ask is that the stock price needs to be able to move a considerable amount in a short time to make the option worth more than zero.

d) Market makers are obligated to make a market in the option, so they have to quote prices even in such an option. The market maker obviously does not want to pay for such an option that is virtually guaranteed to pay off nothing, so that explains the bid price of zero. The ask price might be explained by the market maker wanting to make a small profit, and by some fear that the stock price might rally.

e) The same conclusions as for deep-in-the-money options with extremely short maturity hold—interpretations should be made very cautiously. In academic studies relating to implied volatilities, you therefore often see bounds on moneyness (S/K) and time to maturity when researchers are estimating an implied volatility curve.

Question 23.10.

You can see from the figure below that we observe an implied volatility smile for IBM options. We also learn that the implied volatility curve for the call bid prices is not well behaved.

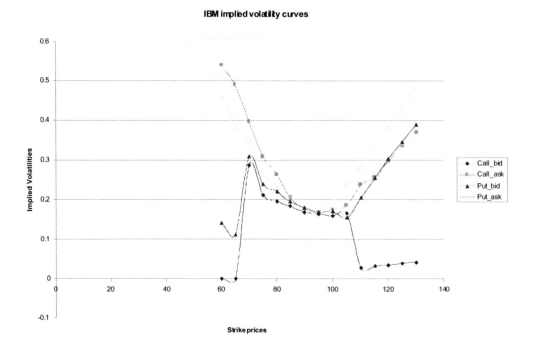

Question 23.12.

Here is a table with all implied volatilities for parts a), b) and c):

Call / Put	Strike	part a)		part b)		part c)	
		bid_implied	ask_implied	bid_implied	ask_implied	bid_implied	ask_implied
C	30	#VALUE!	#VALUE!	58.6%	61.3%	57.2%	60.1%
P	30	14.4%	49.0%	14.1%	44.7%	12.6%	44.7%
C	40	#VALUE!	#VALUE!	41.0%	45.0%	39.5%	43.9%
P	40	34.0%	39.4%	33.8%	36.9%	33.8%	36.9%
C	50	#VALUE!	#VALUE!	32.5%	34.4%	31.5%	33.6%
P	50	31.1%	33.3%	30.8%	32.0%	30.8%	32.0%
C	60	#VALUE!	21.8%	28.5%	29.4%	28.0%	29.0%
P	60	28.4%	29.4%	28.0%	28.6%	28.1%	28.6%
C	70	21.6%	23.6%	25.5%	26.3%	25.2%	26.1%
P	70	26.1%	26.7%	25.7%	26.0%	25.7%	26.0%
C	80	21.3%	22.8%	23.2%	23.9%	23.1%	23.8%
P	80	23.9%	24.6%	23.3%	23.7%	23.4%	23.7%
C	85	21.0%	21.9%	22.4%	22.9%	22.3%	22.8%
P	85	23.1%	23.7%	22.4%	22.7%	22.5%	22.8%
C	90	20.7%	21.3%	21.8%	22.1%	21.8%	22.0%
P	90	22.5%	23.1%	21.7%	22.0%	21.8%	22.1%
C	95	20.1%	20.7%	21.1%	21.3%	21.0%	21.3%
P	95	22.1%	22.6%	21.1%	21.4%	21.2%	21.5%
C	100	19.6%	20.1%	20.3%	20.6%	20.3%	20.6%
P	100	21.8%	22.3%	20.6%	20.9%	20.7%	21.0%
C	110	19.0%	19.6%	19.6%	19.9%	19.6%	19.8%
P	110	21.9%	22.9%	20.1%	20.6%	20.2%	20.7%
C	120	18.1%	19.3%	18.5%	19.1%	18.5%	19.1%
P	120	23.9%	24.7%	21.2%	21.7%	21.4%	21.9%
C	130	18.0%	19.1%	18.3%	18.9%	18.3%	18.9%
P	130	27.2%	28.6%	23.8%	24.7%	24.1%	25.0%
C	140	16.8%	19.5%	17.1%	18.7%	17.1%	18.6%
P	140	31.3%	32.7%	27.7%	28.6%	27.9%	28.9%
C	150	19.2%	22.1%	19.5%	21.2%	19.4%	21.2%
P	150	35.5%	37.0%	31.8%	32.8%	32.1%	33.1%

a)   Note that we cannot calculate implied volatilities for some of the deep-in-the-money call options.

b)   We have to find all dividends for 2004 and discount them appropriately. Note that we make the assumption here that we had perfect foresight about the dividends: We use dividends for all of 2004, although we are calculating option prices on January 12th, 2004. This is in real life not possible, and you would have to make the assumption that past dividends are a good proxy for future dividends.

We have:

	amount	date	days to maturity	discounted at 2%
Div1	0.16	3/10/2004	58	0.159492
Div2	0.18	6/10/2004	150	0.178527
Div3	0.18	9/10/2004	242	0.177629
Div4	0.18	12/10/2004	333	0.176745
Total				0.692393

We correct the IBM stock price of $91.55 by $0.6924 to $90.8576, and use that price in the volatility calculations. Most notably, you should see that you can now calculate implied volatilities for the low-strike options from part a).

c)   We have to calculate an annualized dividend rate. In 2003, we had the following dividend payments:

date	amount
3/10/2003	0.15
6/10/2003	0.16
9/10/2003	0.16
12/10/2003	0.16
Total	0.63

We obtain a dividend yield of 0.69% (0.63 / 91.55). The implied volatilities are quite close for parts b) and c), so it does not make a big difference which dividend adjustment model we use.

d)   Look at the following figure:

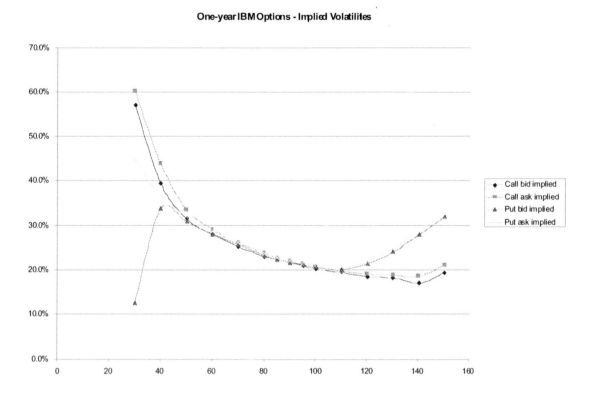

One-year IBM Options - Implied Volatilites

There is some evidence of a smile in put options, although for call options, it looks more like a smirk.

Question 23.14.

	$5-step	strike in [60,200]	$1-step	$10-step
forward price	108.329	108.329	108.329	108.329
K0	105	105	108	100
sum(put-term)	0.0467	0.0459	0.0489	0.0413
sum(call-term)	0.0431	0.0428	0.0410	0.0488
F(0,T) adjustment	0.00101	0.00101	0.00001	0.00694
Sigma2Vix	0.089	0.088	0.090	0.083
Sigma Vix	0.298	0.296	0.300	0.288

We know that the true implied volatility is equal to 30%—after all, we created the prices! We learn from the table that the wider the dispersion of strike prices, the more accurate the calculation of VIX (Compare columns 1 and 2). We also learn that the finer the grid of strike prices, the more accurate the calculation of VIX. In fact, we know that the formula is true for continuous strike prices, but the $1 approximation works already very accurately up to the fourth decimal. You can see that the $10 distance in strikes (column 4) does not work as well—we are 1.2 percentage points away from the true implied volatility.

Question 23.16.

This is a difficult exercise. The most difficult part is to set up the spreadsheet for the infinite sum in the formula 21.60. Note that we divide by factorial(i), so that the weight decays very quickly. You should be alright to sum up to a value of $i = 50$, and ignore all other terms. Also note from chapter 19 that

$$k = e^{\alpha_j} - 1$$

In order to set up the spreadsheet, enter in column A the indicator i ($i = 1$ to 50), define in column B the exponential weights, and in columns C to W, enter the strike prices from 50 to 150. Then, for each strike, sum over all 50 rows.

Stop reading here now if you did not find the solution and try again, it is worth it.

Here are the values for the first four strike prices for the implied volatility (using the BSCallImpVol function that comes with the spreadsheet), backed out from the generated Merton Jump Diffusion prices:

K	50	55	60	65
a_j = −0.2, s_j = 0.3	0.3457	0.3334	0.3248	0.3190
a_j = −0.4, s_j = 0.3	0.3623	0.3464	0.3348	0.3266
a_j = −0.1, s_j = 0.3	0.3382	0.3276	0.3205	0.3159
a_j = −0.2, s_j = 0.1	0.3183	0.3137	0.3107	0.3086
a_j = −0.2, s_j = 0.4	0.3645	0.3475	0.3352	0.3268
lambda = 0.01	0.3273	0.3187	0.3133	0.3099
lambda = 0.05	0.3831	0.3663	0.3530	0.3428

The implied volatility curve for the different prices looks like this:

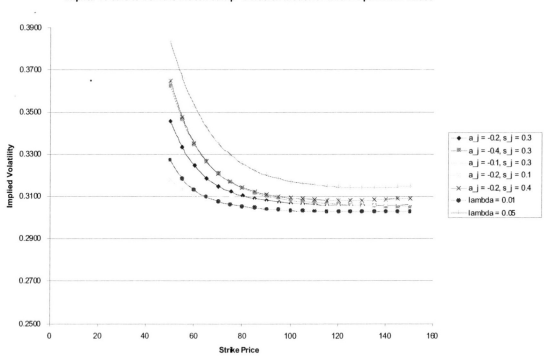

The steepest curve is created for lambda = 0.05, the flattest "smirk" is created when sigma_j = 0.1.

Question 23.18.

Here is a graph of the implied volatility estimations:

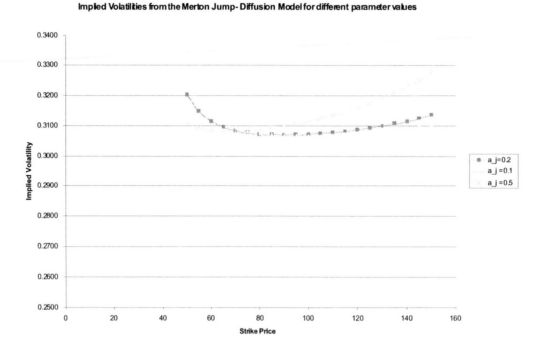

The main point is that the implied volatility smirk can "smirk" in the other direction if we make the jump magnitude positive enough (see the upwards sloping curve for alpha(j) = 0.5.

Question 23.20.

We get the following prices from the CEV model:

	$t = 0.25$	$t = 0.5$	$t = 1$	$t = 2$
60	41.1881	42.3589	44.6969	49.2451
65	36.2882	37.581	40.2262	45.3347
70	31.3963	32.8632	35.8988	41.6058
75	26.5425	28.2761	31.7775	38.0881
80	21.8053	23.9145	27.9192	34.8017
85	17.3231	19.8784	24.3671	31.7566
90	13.2674	16.2511	21.147	28.9545
95	9.7874	13.084	18.2674	26.3904
100	6.9632	10.392	15.7222	24.0543
105	4.791	8.1581	13.4945	21.9332
110	3.1997	6.3422	11.5602	20.012
115	2.0827	4.8916	9.8913	18.275
120	1.3266	3.7495	8.4585	16.7062
125	0.8302	2.8606	7.2331	15.2902
130	0.5122	2.1752	6.1879	14.0125
135	0.3125	1.6505	5.298	12.8593
140	0.1891	1.2509	4.5412	11.818

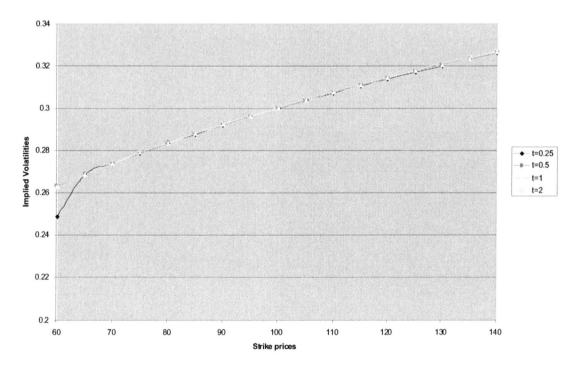

Implied Volatilties from CEV model for beta = 3

The resulting implied volatility curve is now upward sloping.

Chapter 24
Interest Rate Models

Question 24.2.

a)   The two year forward price is $F = P(0, 3)/P(0, 2) = .7722/.8495 = .90901$.

b)   Since $FP(0, 2) = P(0, 3)$ the first input into the formula will be .7722. The present value of the strike price is $.9P(0, 2) = .9 \times .8495 = .76455$. We can use this as the strike with no interest rate; we could also use a strike of .9 with an interest rate equal to the 2 year yield. Either way the option is worth

$$BSCall(.7722, .76455, .105, 0, 2, 0) = \$0.0494 \tag{1}$$

c)   Using put call parity for futures options,

$$p = c + KP(0, 2) - FP(0, 2) = .0494 + .76455 - .7722 = \$0.4175. \tag{2}$$

d)   The caplet is worth 1.11 two year put options with strike $1/1.11 = .9009$. The no interest formula will use $(.9009)(.8495) = .7653$ as the strike. The caplet has a value of

$$1.11 BSPut(.7722, .7653, .105, 0, 2, 0) = \$0.0468. \tag{3}$$

Question 24.4.

A flat yield curve implies the two bond prices are $P_1 = e^{-.08(3)} = .78663$ and $P_2 = e^{-.08(6)} = .61878$. If we have purchased the three year bond, the duration hedge is a position of

$$N = -\frac{1}{2}\frac{P_1}{P_2} = -\frac{1}{2}e^{3(.08)} = -.63562 \tag{4}$$

in the six year bond. Notice the total cost of this strategy is

$$V_{8\%} = .78663 - .63562(.61878) = .39332 \tag{5}$$

which implies we will owe $.39332e^{.08/365} = .39341$ in one day. If yields rise to 8.25%, our portfolio will have a value

$$V_{8.25\%} = e^{-.0825(3-1/365)} - .63562e^{-.0825(6-1/365)} = .39338. \tag{6}$$

If yields fall to 7.75%, the value will be

$$V_{7.75\%} = e^{-.0775(3-1/365)} - .63562e^{-.0775(6-1/365)} = .39338. \tag{7}$$

Either way we lose .00003. This is a binomial version of the impossibility of a no arbitrage flat (stochastic) yield curve.

Question 24.6.

Note that the interest rate risk premium of zero implies $\phi = 0$.

a)   Beginning with the CIR model and using equation (23.37),

$$\gamma = \sqrt{a^2 + 2\sigma^2} = \sqrt{.2^2 + 2(.44721)^2} = .66332. \tag{8}$$

Let A_2 and B_2 be the 2 year bond's A and B term in equation (23.37). Then

$$A_2 = \left(\frac{2\gamma e^{.2+\gamma}}{(.2+\gamma)\left(e^{2\gamma} - 1\right) + 2\gamma} \right)^{.04/.44721^2} = .96718 \tag{9}$$

and

$$B_2 = \frac{2\left(e^{2\gamma} - 1\right)}{(.2+\gamma)\left(e^{2\gamma} - 1\right) + 2\gamma} = 1.4897. \tag{10}$$

This gives a price of the two year bond equal to

$$P(0,2) = .96718e^{-1.4897(.05)} = .89776. \tag{11}$$

The delta is $P_r = -B_2 P(0,2) = -1.4897(.89776) = -1.3374$ and the gamma is $P_{rr} = B_2^2 P(0,2) = 1.4897^2(.89776) = 1.9923$. Similar analysis for the ten year bond will yield a price of $P(0,10) = .6107$, a delta of -1.4119, and a gamma of 3.2643. The "true" duration of the bonds should be $-P_r/P$ which equal 1.49 and 2.31 (respectively) quite different from 2 and 10 years. The "true" convexity should be P_{rr}/P which equals 2.22 and 5.35; the traditional convexities are $P_{yy}/P = 4$ and 100.

Using similar notation for the Vasicek model and equation (23.24) the two year bond price is derived from the components

$$\bar{r} = .1 - 0.5\left(.1^2\right)/.2^2 = -.025, \tag{12}$$

$$B_2 = \left(1 - e^{-2(.2)}\right)/.2 = 1.6484, \tag{13}$$

163

and

$$A_2 = e^{-.025(1.6484-2)-.16484^2/.8} = .97514. \tag{14}$$

The two year bond will be worth $P(0, 2) = .97514e^{-1.6484(.05)} = .89799$. As in the CIR analysis, the delta will be $P_r = -B_2 P(0, 2) = -1.6484(.89799) = -1.4802$ and a gamma of $P_{rr} = B_2^2 P(0, 2) = 1.6484^2(.89799) = 2.44$. Similarly, the price of the 10 year bond is .735, the delta is -3.1776, and the gamma is 13.74. The "true" durations $-P_r/P$ are 1.65 and 4.32 are substantially different from 2 and 10. The convexity measures P_{rr}/P which equal 2.72 and 18.694 are also quite different from 4 and 100.

b)   The duration hedge will use a position of

$$N_{duration} = -\frac{2}{10}\frac{P(0, 2)}{P(0, 10)} = -.2(.89799)/.735 = -.24435. \tag{15}$$

The delta hedge is

$$N_{delta} = -\frac{P_r(0, 2)}{P_r(0, 10)} = -\frac{1.4802}{3.177} = -.4658. \tag{16}$$

The duration hedged portfolio has a cost of $.89799 - .24435(.735) = .71839$ and the delta hedge costs $.89799 - .4658(.735) = .55563$. The one day standard deviation for r will be $.05 \pm .1/\sqrt{365}$. In the "up" scenario the bond prices will become $P_2 = .8904$ and $P_{10} = .7186$. The return in the up scenario for the two hedges are

$$return_{duration} = .8904 - .24435(.7186) - .71839e^{.05/365} = -.00368 \tag{17}$$

and

$$return_{delta} = .8904 - .4658(.7186) - .55563e^{.05/365} = -.00003. \tag{18}$$

In the "down" scenario the bond prices will be $P_2 = .905895$ and $P_{10} = .751818$. The return in the down scenario for the two hedges are

$$return_{duration} = .905895 - .24435(.751818) - .71839e^{.05/365} = .0037 \tag{19}$$

and

$$return_{delta} = .905895 - .4658(.751818) - .55563e^{.05/365} = -.00009. \tag{20}$$

The delta hedge error is significantly smaller (in absolute terms) in both scenarios.

c)   The one day standard deviation for the CIR model is $\sigma_{CIR}\sqrt{r/365} = 5.2342 \times 10^{-3}$ which is, by design, the same as part b). The duration hedge is

$$N_{duration} = -\frac{2}{10}\frac{P(0,2)}{P(0,10)} = -.2\frac{.89776}{.6107} = -.29401. \tag{21}$$

which has a total cost of $.89776 - .29401\,(.6107) = .71821$. The delta hedge is

$$N_{delta} = -\frac{P_r(0,2)}{P_r(0,10)} = -\frac{1.3374}{1.4119} = -.94723. \tag{22}$$

which has a total cost of $.89776 - .94723\,(.6107) = .3193$. If r rises by the one day standard deviation, the bond prices will be $P_2 = .89092$ and $P_{10} = .603436$. This leads to "up" returns of

$$return_{duration} = .89092 - .29401\,(.6034) - .71821e^{.05/365} = -.0048 \tag{23}$$

and

$$return_{delta} = .89092 - .94723\,(.6034) - .3193e^{.05/365} = -6.42 \times 10^{-6}. \tag{24}$$

If the short term rate falls by the one day standard deviation, the bond prices will be $P_2 = .9049$ and $P_{10} = .6182$, leading to "down" returns of

$$return_{duration} = .9049 - .2940\,(.6182) - .71821e^{.05/365} = .0048. \tag{25}$$

and

$$return_{delta} = .9049 - .94723\,(.6182) - .3193e^{.05/365} = -2.13 \times 10^{-5}. \tag{26}$$

Without rounding errors the return is closer to -6×10^{-6}.

Question 24.8.

Instead of one long equation we will work backwards. In year 3, the four year bond is worth the same value as the 1-year bond in the terminal nodes of Figure 24.6. In year two the bond will be worth three possible values, $.8321\left(\frac{.8331+.8644}{2}\right) = .70624$, $.8798\left(\frac{.8644+.8906}{2}\right) = .77202$, and $.9153\frac{(.8906+.9123)}{2} = .8251$. In year one, the bond will be worth two possible values, $.8832\left(\frac{.70624+.77202}{2}\right) = .6528$ or $.9023\left(\frac{.77202+.8251}{2}\right) = .72054$. Finally, the current value is the discounted expected value

$$P(0,4) = .9091\left(\frac{.6528+.72054}{2}\right) = .6243. \tag{27}$$

Question 24.10.

The value of the year-2 cap payment has been shown to be $V_2 = 1.958$. We must add to this the value of the year-3 cap payment and the value of the year-1 cap payment. In year 2, the year-3 cap payment will be worth three possible values: $.8321 \left(\frac{6.689 + 3.184}{2} \right) = 4.1077$, $.8798 \left(\frac{3.184 + .25}{2} \right) = 1.5106$, or $.9153 (.125) = .11441$. In year 1, the year-3 cap payment will be worth two possible values: $.8832 \left(\frac{4.1077 + 1.5106}{2} \right) = 2.481$ or $.9023 \left(\frac{1.5106 + .11441}{2} \right) = .73312$. Hence the year-3 cap payment has a current value of

$$V_3 = .9091 \left(\frac{2.481 + .73312}{2} \right) = 1.461. \tag{28}$$

The year-1 cap payment has a value of $V_1 = .9091 \left(\frac{1.078}{2} \right) = .49$. Summing the three we have

$$V_1 + V_2 + V_3 = .49 + 1.958 + 1.461 = 3.909. \tag{29}$$

Question 24.12.

See Table Two on the next page for the bond prices which are the same for the two trees. The one year bonds are simply $1/(1 + r)$ where r is the short rate from the given trees. For the two year bonds we can solve recursively with formulas such as $B(0, 2) = B(0, 1) \times \left[\frac{B(0,1)_u + B(0,1)_d}{2} \right]$ where $B(0, 1)$ is the node's 1 year bond and $B(0, 1)_u$ and $B(0, 1)_d$ are the one year bond prices at the next node. Once we have two year bonds, three year bond values can be given by $B(0, 3) = B(0, 1) \times \left[\frac{B(0,2)_u + B(0,2)_d}{2} \right]$ and similarly for the four and 5 year bonds.

Question 24.14.

See Table Four on the next page for the numerical answers to parts a) and b). Let $r_f(i)$ and $r_e(i)$ be the one period forward rate for borrowing at time i.

a)   Note the forward rates only depend on the initial bond prices; for example, $r_f(2) = B(0, 1)/B(0, 2) - 1 = .925926/.849454 - 1 = 9.0025\%$. This immediately implies the yield volatilities do not affect these forward rates.

b)   These rates were computed by formulas such as

$$r_e(2) = \frac{r_u + r_d}{2} \tag{30}$$

and

$$r_e(3) = \frac{1}{B(0, 2)} \left(\frac{1}{2(1 + r_d)} \frac{r_{dd} + r_{du}}{2} + \frac{1}{2(1 + r_u)} \frac{r_{du} + r_{uu}}{2} \right). \tag{31}$$

Table Two (Problem 24.12)

Tree #1

0.08	0.07676	0.0817	0.07943	0.07552
	0.10362	0.10635	0.09953	0.09084
		0.13843	0.12473	0.10927
			0.1563	0.13143
				0.15809

One Year Bond Prices

0.925926	0.928712	0.924471	0.926415	0.929783
	0.906109	0.903873	0.90948	0.916725
		0.878403	0.889102	0.901494
			0.864827	0.883837
				0.863491

Two Year Bond Prices

0.849454	0.849002	0.848615	0.855316
	0.807468	0.812845	0.826816
		0.770328	0.793671
			0.755569

Three Year Bond Prices

0.766885	0.771509	0.777541
	0.717264	0.732357
		0.680428

Four Year Bond Prices

| **0.689247** | 0.70113 |
| | 0.640069 |

Five Year Bond Price

0.620926

Tree #2

0.08	0.08112	0.08749	0.08261	0.07284
	0.09908	0.10689	0.10096	0.08907
		0.1306	0.12338	0.10891
			0.15078	0.13317
				0.16283

0.925926	0.924967	0.919549	0.923694	0.932105
	0.909852	0.903432	0.908298	0.918215
		0.884486	0.890171	0.901786
			0.868976	0.88248
				0.859971

0.849453	0.843098	0.842303	0.854564
	0.81337	0.812397	0.826552
		0.77797	0.794151
			0.757074

0.766884	0.765271	0.772934
	0.7235	0.732097
		0.686018

| **0.689246** | 0.696052 |
| | 0.645138 |

0.620921

Table Four (Problem 24.14)

1 year

forward rate	American	European	Difference
Year 2	9.002%	9.019%	0.017%
Year 3	10.767%	10.803%	0.036%
Year 4	11.264%	11.308%	0.044%
Year 5	11.003%	11.041%	0.037%

Year 3 European Calculations

| 0.0917689 | 0.087322 |
| | 0.110899 |

0.10803279

Year 4 European Calculations

0.08671898	0.085475	0.082722
	0.101838	0.101351
0.11307958		0.123429

Year 5 European Calculations

0.07609656	0.077625	0.077682	0.077059
	0.086744	0.089484	0.090998
0.11040541		0.101981	0.107003
			0.125192

1 year

forward rate	American	European	Difference
Year 2	9.003%	9.003%	0.000%
Year 3	10.767%	10.788%	0.021%
Year 4	11.264%	11.299%	0.035%
Year 5	11.004%	11.048%	0.044%

Year 3 European Calculations

| 0.0916379 | 0.089898 |
| | 0.10804 |

0.10787872

Year 4 European Calculations

0.08664816	0.085901	0.084401
	0.101259	0.101338
0.11298736		0.121245

Year 5 European Calculations

0.07614931	0.076312	0.07572	0.074778
	0.08817	0.089286	0.089912
0.11048209		0.104526	0.107746
			0.128608

c)   From Table Four, we see that the difference between the two settlement styles is larger for the high volatility tree (#1) for the year 2 and 3 forward rates. In addition, the difference is larger for the later years. In looking at the short rate trees we see that the short rate tree #1 has a lower dispersion in year 4 (ranging from 7.55% to 15.81%) than it does in tree #2 (ranging from 7.28% to 16.28%). This causes the difference for the 5 year rates to be more pronounced for tree #2.

Chapter 25
Value at Risk

Question 25.2.

A 95% VaR uses $Z_1 = -1.645$ and the 99% VaR uses $Z_2 = -2.326$. Given the horizon h (in years), the value of 10 million will be $10e^{(\alpha-\sigma^2/2)h+\sigma\sqrt{h}Z_i}$ million. Table One shows these values as well as the loss (VaR).

Table One (Problem 25.2)

95%

Values	1 day	10 day	20 day
A	9,747,824	9,242,241	8,960,529
B	9,622,055	8,866,025	8,445,521
Loss (VaR)	1 day	10 day	20 day
A	252,176	757,759	1,039,471
B	377,945	1,133,975	1,554,479

99%

Values	1 day	10 day	20 day
A	9,644,067	8,934,714	8,541,801
B	9,468,836	8,427,213	7,860,500
Loss (VaR)			
A	355,933	1,065,286	1,458,199
B	531,164	1,572,787	2,139,500

Question 25.4.

The portfolio mean is $\alpha_p = 16.3\%$ and the standard deviation is $\sigma_p = 28.65\%$. Letting h be the holding period, there is a 95% (or 99%) chance the value of the portfolio will exceed

$$\$10m \times \left[1 + \alpha_p h + \sigma_p \sqrt{h} Z_i\right] \tag{1}$$

where $Z_1 = -1.645$ (95%) and $Z_2 = -2.326$ (99%). See Table Three for the numerical answers.

Table Three (Problem 25.4)

Values	1 day	10 day	20 day
95%	9,757,785	9,264,584	8,986,124
99%	9,655,581	8,941,387	8,529,054
Loss (VaR)	1 day	10 day	20 day
95%	242,215	735,416	1,013,876
99%	344,419	1,058,613	1,470,946

Question 25.6.

The 100,000 105-strike one year put options have a premium of \$1,026,694.90, hence $W = 11,026,694$. The delta (per share) is -0.3997. Using equations (24.10) and (24.11), we obtain

$$R_p = \frac{.15 \times 100}{W}(100000\,(1 - .3997)) = .081656 \tag{2}$$

and

$$\sigma_p = \frac{100^2 \times .3^2}{W^2}(100000\,(1 - .3997))^2 = .16331. \tag{3}$$

Table Five shows the 6 VaR values using the normal approximation.

Table Five (Problem 25.6)

	95%			99%		
	1 day	10 day	20 day	1 day	10 day	20 day
Value	10,874,121	10,561,083	10,382,670	10,809,886	10,357,951	10,095,399
Loss (VaR)	152,574	465,612	644,025	216,809	668,743	931,296

Question 25.8.

We first do the problem analytically; since we have written options we receive the premiums which is \$1,571,210. It is virtually impossible for S to fall enough in a week for there to be a loss ($Z \approx -5.64$). The 95% 10-day VaR is therefore the loss when $Z = 1.645$; with this value the option position will be \$1,901,066 which is a loss of \$329,856. Monte Carlo simulations should confirm this.

The delta of our position is $-100000\,(-.22128 + .539417) = -31814$. If we use the delta approximation, we could use a normal approximation with return

$$R_p = \frac{100000}{1571210}.15\,(100)\,(.318135) = 30.372\% \tag{4}$$

and variance

$$\sigma_p^2 = \frac{100^2\,(31814)^2\,.3^2}{1571210^2} = 36.899\%. \tag{5}$$

Using a normal approximation, the value of our portfolio would be

$$W_h = -1571210\left(1 + R_p\frac{10}{365} + \sigma_p\sqrt{\frac{10}{365}}Z\right). \tag{6}$$

Our profit is $W_h + 1571210$. If $Z = 1.645$, the profit will be negative; this amounts to a 95% 10-day VaR of $272,947 which is much less than the true VaR of $329,856. This large error is due to the linear approximation of a highly non-linear payoff. The payoff is similar to Figure 24.3. The negative delta of -31814 underestimates the true loss due to a negative gamma.

Question 25.10.

As in problem 25.8, the loss occurs when the stock price rises, i.e. $Z = 1.645$. At this value the portfolio is worth $-1,901,066$. The conditional expected value of the portfolio should be approximately 2.025m leading to tail VaR that is approximately $454,000. The simulation method is to sort the portfolio values and then take the average only of those simulations where the value is greater than 1.9m.

Question 25.12.

Since $8 = \frac{2}{3}7 + \frac{1}{3}10$, interpolation implies

$$y_8 = \frac{2}{3}(.06) + \frac{1}{3}(.065) = .06167 \tag{7}$$

$$\sigma_8 = \frac{2}{3}(.10) + \frac{1}{3}(.095) = .09833. \tag{8}$$

The yield being 6.167% implies the bond position is worth $10e^{-.06167(8)} = \$6.1059$m. Using these values, the 10-day 95% VaR is

$$\$6.1059\text{m} \times \left(1 + .09833 \times 8 \times \sqrt{\frac{10}{365}} \times (-1.645)\right) - \$6.1059\text{m} = -\$1.31\text{m} \tag{9}$$

and a 10-day 99% VaR of

$$\$6.1509\text{m} \times \left(1 + .09833 \times 8 \times \sqrt{\frac{10}{365}} \times (-2.326)\right) - \$6.1509\text{m} = -\$1.85\text{m}. \tag{10}$$

Chapter 26
Credit Risk

Question 26.2.

Using the formulas of the main text, we can calculate the following values for the yield, the probability of default, and the expected loss given default for all times to maturity:

Years to Maturity	Yield	Prob Default	Recovery	Expected Loss Given Default	Approx
1	0.215502281	0.5	74.65543	0.253445658	0.206723
2	0.169925969	0.5	67.07878	0.329212215	0.162303
3	0.150053883	0.5	62.09065	0.379093545	0.143182
4	0.138376782	0.5	58.35039	0.416496097	0.132062
5	0.130513667	0.5	55.36063	0.446393746	0.124639
10	0.111591282	0.5	45.8246	0.541753977	0.107088
20	0.099109428	0.5	36.47327	0.63526726	0.095882

Note that the probability of default is constant for the parameter values chosen. The last column of the above table shows the approximations. They work remarkably well.

Question 26.4.

a)   We can calculate for a maturity value of $80

mat val	80	80	80	80	80	80	80
Time to mat	1	2	3	4	5	10	20
Bond price	69.453	61.391	54.921	49.458	44.728	27.965	11.661
Yield	0.141	0.132	0.125	0.120	0.116	0.105	0.096
Prob default	0.288	0.347	0.374	0.390	0.401	0.430	0.450
Expected recovery	63.489	57.044	52.754	49.526	46.940	38.688	30.614
Expected loss given default	0.206	0.287	0.341	0.381	0.413	0.516	0.617

b)   For a maturity value of $120, we obtain:

mat val	120	120	120	120	120	120	120
Time to mat	1	2	3	4	5	10	20
Bond price	88.145	78.590	70.773	64.077	58.214	36.989	15.711
Yield	0.309	0.212	0.176	0.157	0.145	0.118	0.102
Prob default	0.676	0.626	0.604	0.590	0.581	0.557	0.541
Expected recovery	83.723	75.660	70.264	66.186	62.912	52.390	41.971
Expected loss given default	0.302	0.369	0.414	0.448	0.476	0.563	0.650

c)   For a maturity value of $80, the probability of default is increasing, and for a maturity value of $120, the probability of default is decreasing. If the maturity value is $80, we start out with a bond obligation that is well below our current asset threshold. Within a short time to maturity it is more unlikely that the asset value decreases below the threshold of $80, but the likelihood increases with time to maturity. Conversely, with a maturity value of $120, we have a debt obligation that is considerably higher than our current asset value. The initial probability of default is very high. The longer we allow the asset price to develop, the more likely it is that it drifts upward, and that the assets increase beyond the threshold of $120.

Question 26.6.

We can calculate the following values for the bond prices, yields, and expected losses for the model with and without jump risk:

	Without jump risk	With jump risk
mat val	110	100
time to mat	5	5
Bond price	55.278	47.098
Yield	0.1376	0.1506

Incorporating jump risk makes the bond less valuable, and thus increases the yield.

Question 26.8.

Using the different maturities, we obtain the following yields:

Time to mat	1	2	3	4	5	10	20
Equity	11.855	21.407	29.185	35.751	41.367	60.065	75.500
Bond price	88.145	78.593	70.815	64.249	58.633	39.935	24.500
Yield	0.309	0.212	0.176	0.156	0.143	0.110	0.079
Terminal Prob default	0.654	0.521	0.420	0.344	0.287	0.144	0.062
intermediary Probability of default	0.011	0.053	0.093	0.126	0.153	0.234	0.304
Total probability of default	0.665	0.574	0.513	0.470	0.440	0.378	0.366

We can see that the yields are continuously decreasing with maturity. The probabilities of default are going down, suggesting that the bond becomes progressively less risky.

Question 26.10.

The answer to these questions can be read directly from the transition matrix:

4-year matrix	F	FF	FFF
F	0.72089	0.211302	0.067809
FF	0.401668	0.507982	0.090351
FFF	0.345313	0.470535	0.184153

An FF rating is retained with 50.8% probability; a rating change happens with 49.2% probability.

An FFF rating is retained with 18.4% probability, an FFF rated company changes its rating with 81.6% probability.

Question 26.12.

Following the procedure in the main textbook, we can write:

				Bond Payoff		
Number of Defaults	Proba	Total Payoff	Tranche1	Tranche2	Tranche3
0	0.9	300	160	50	90
1	0	240	160	50	30
2	0	180	160	20	0
3	0.1	120	120	0	0
Price			146.9153	42.3794	76.28293
Yield			0.085318	0.165361	0.165361
Default probability			0.1	0.1	0.1
Average recovery rate			0.75	0	0

Question 26.14.

Using the same methodology as before, but extending the number of bonds in the portfolio, we can calculate for 5, 10, 20, and 50 bond portfolios:

	1st-to-default	2nd-to-default	5th-to-default
Expected Payoff	75.39228	95.11315	99.99402
Price	71.00178	89.57419	94.17082
Yield	0.342465	0.110103	0.06006

	1st-to-default	2nd-to-default	10th-to-default
Expected Payoff	60.33097	83.77231	100
Price	56.81757	78.89379	94.17645
Yield	0.565325	0.237068	0.06

	1st-to-default	2nd-to-default	20th-to-default
Expected Payoff	46.48988	62.85515	100
Price	43.78252	59.19475	94.17645
Yield	0.825936	0.524337	0.06

	1st-to-default	2nd-to-default	50th-to-default
Expected Payoff	40.29309	41.79444	100
Price	37.9466	39.36052	94.17645
Yield	0.96899	0.932407	0.06

You can see a dramatic increase in the yields of the first- and second-to-default bonds the more bonds are included in the portfolio. However, for the Nth-to-default bond, there is little variation in the yield. Already with five included bonds, it is virtually risk-free, i.e. the probability of all five uncorrelated bonds defaulting at the same time is almost zero.